COLLECTED POEMS

COLLECTED POEMS

Jack Gilbert

ALFRED A. KNOPF

NEW YORK

2012

THIS IS A BORZOI BOOK
PUBLISHED BY ALFRED A. KNOPF

www.aaknopf.com

Knopf, Borzoi Books, and the colophon are registered
trademarks of Random House, Inc.

Library of Congress Cataloging-in-Publication Data
Gilbert, Jack, [date]
[Poems, Selections]
Collected poems / by Jack Gilbert. — 1st ed.
p. cm.
ISBN 978-0-307-26968-3
I. Title.
PS3557.I34217A6 2012
811'.54 — dc23
2011025743

Jacket image: *Jack, 1960,* woodcut by
Gianna Gelmetti (1937–2010)
Jacket design by Abby Weintraub

Manufactured in the United States of America
First Edition

For Gianna Gelmetti, Michiko Nogami, and Linda Gregg

CONTENTS

VIEWS OF

JEOPARDY

[1962]

IN DISPRAISE OF POETRY

When the King of Siam disliked a courtier,
he gave him a beautiful white elephant.
The miracle beast deserved such ritual
that to care for him properly meant ruin.
Yet to care for him improperly was worse.
It appears the gift could not be refused.

PERSPECTIVE HE WOULD MUTTER GOING TO BED

For Robert Duncan

"Perspective," he would mutter, going to bed.
"Oh che dolce cosa è questa
prospettiva." Uccello. Bird.

And I am as greedy of her, that the black
horse of the literal world might come
directly on me. Perspective. A place

to stand. To receive. A place to go
into from. The earth by language.

Who can imagine antelope silent
under the night rain, the Gulf
at Biloxi at night else? I remember

in Mexico a man and a boy painting
an adobe house magenta and crimson
who thought they were painting it red. Or pretty.

So neither saw the brown mountains
move to manage that great house.

The horse wades in the city of grammar.

ELEPHANTS

For Jean McLean

The great foreign trees and turtles burn
as Pharos, demanding my house continue ahead.
In my blood all night the statues counsel return.

I walk my mornings in hope of tigers that yearn
for absolute orchards and the grace of rivers, but instead
the great foreign trees and turtles burn

down my life, driving my hands from the fern
of tenderness that crippled and stopped the Roman bed
in my blood. All night the statues counsel return

even so, gesturing toward Cézanne and stern
styles of voyaging broken and blessed. "It is the dead
the great foreign trees and turtles burn

to momentary brilliance," they say. "Such as earn
their heat only from the violation they wed."
In my blood all night the statues counsel return

to the measure that passionate Athenian dancers learn.
But though I assent, the worn elephants that bred
the great foreign trees and turtles burn
in my blood all night the statues, counsel, return.

AND SHE WAITING

Always I have been afraid
of this moment:
of the return to love
with perspective.

I see these breasts
with the others.
I touch this mouth
and the others.
I command this heart
as the others.
I know exactly
what to say.

Innocence has gone
out of me.
The song.
The song, suddenly,
has gone out
of me.

IT MAY BE NO ONE SHOULD BE OPENED

You know I am serious about the whales.
Their moving vast through that darkness,
silent.
It is intolerable.
Or Crivelli, with his fruit.
The Japanese.
Or the white flesh of casaba melons
always in darkness.
That darkness unopened from the beginning.
The small emptiness at the middle
in darkness.
As virgins.
The landscape unlighted.
Lighted by me.
Lighted as my hands
in the darkroom
pinching film on the spindle
in absolute dark.
The work difficult
and my hands soon large and brilliant.
Virgins.
Whales.
Darkness and Lauds.
But it may be that no one should be opened.
The deer come back to the feeding station
at the suddenly open season.
The girls find second loves.
Semele was blasted
looking on the whale
in even his lesser panoply.
It was the excellent Socrates ruined Athens.
Now you have fallen crazy

and I have run away.
It's not the dreams.
It's this love of you
that grows in me
malignant.

HOUSE ON THE CALIFORNIA MOUNTAIN

one   All at once these owls
waiting under the white eaves
my burrowing heart

one   In your bright climate
three machines and a tiger
promote my still life

one   All this rainless month
hearing the terrible sound
of apples at night

one   Above the bright bay
a white bird tilting to dark
for only me now

one   You sent loud young men
to collect your well-known things
it may be kindness

one   The pear tree is dead
our garden full of winter
only silence grows

one   A tin bird turning
across the tarnished water
for not even me

one   Always I will live
in that Green Castle with rain
and my ugly love

MYSELF CONSIDERED AS THE MONSTER IN THE FOREGROUND

This monster inhabits no classical world.
Nor Sienese. He ranges the Village
and the Colosseum of Times Square.
Foraging heavily through Provincetown,
through the Hub, Denver, and the Vieux Carré,
He comes at last to the last city—
past the limbo of Berkeley to North Beach
and the nine parts of Market Street.

Having evaded the calm bright castle,
so beautiful, and fatal, on the nearby hill,
the beast goes persistently toward purgatory
as his special journey to salvation. No girl-
princess will kiss this dragon to prince.
And as always, the hero with the vacant face
who charges on the ignorant horse to preserve
the Aristotelian suburb is harmless.

Safe and helpless, the monster must fashion
his own blessing or doom. He goes down,
as it is in the nature of serpents to go down,
but goes down with a difference, down to the mountain
that he must and would eventually ascend.
Yet monster he is, with a taste for decay.
Who feeds by preference on novelty and shock;
on the corrupt and vulgar, the abnormal and sick.

He feeds with pleasure in the electric swamp
of Fosters with its night tribe of Saint Jude.
Delights in the dirty movies of the arcades
and the Roman crowds of blatant girls
with their fat breasts and smug faces.
The beast rejoices in fires and fanatics,

and the revelations gestured by the drunk
stunned by the incredible drug store.

Still it is a beast bent on grace.
A monster going down hoping to prove
a monster by emphasis and for a time—
knowing how many are feeding and crying
they are saintly dragons on their way to God,
looking for the breakthrough to heaven.
But the monster goes down as required. O pray
for this foolish, maybe chosen beast.

IN PERUGINO WE HAVE SOMETIMES SEEN
OUR COUNTRY

For Gianna

In Perugino we have sometimes seen our country.
Incidental, beyond the Madonna, the mild hills
and the valley we have always almost remembered,
the light which explains our secret conviction
of exile. That light, that valley, those hills,
that country where people finally touch
as we would touch, reaching with hand and body
and mouth, crying, and do not meet.
Those perfect small trees of loneliness,
dark with my longing against the light.

A POEM FOR THE FIN DU MONDE MAN

I
In the beginning
there were six brown dragons
whose names were
Salt, Salt, Salt, Salt,
Bafflebar
and Kenneth Rexroth.

II
They were everything and identical and formless.
Being everything, they lived, of necessity,
inside each other.
Being formless, they were, of necessity,
dull.
And the world was without savor.

III
Then the fourth dragon,
whose name was Salt,
died,
or lost interest
and stopped.
So anxiety came into the world.

IV
Which so troubled the first dragon
that he coiled his body to make space
and filled it with elm trees
and paradichlorobenzene
and moons
and a fish called Humuhumunukunukuapua'a.

V

But nothing would stay fresh.
The elm trees bore winter.
The moons kept going down.
The Humuhumunukunukuapua'a kept floating to the top
    of the tank.
And he found there was no end to the odor of
paradichlorobenzene.

VI

So the second and sixth dragons
decided to help
and to demonstrate the correct way
of making things.
But everything somehow came out men and
    women.
And the world was in real trouble.

VII

In alarm, the dragons quit.
But it was too late.
All over the world men were talking about the elms.
Or calculating about the moon.
Or writing songs about the Humuhumunukunukuapua'a.
And the women sat around repeating over and over
    how they absolutely could not stand the smell
    of paradichlorobenzene.

If you're a dragon with nothing to do, LOOK OUT.

RAIN

Suddenly this defeat.
This rain.
The blues gone gray
and yellow
a terrible amber.
In the cold streets
your warm body.
In whatever room
your warm body.
Among all the people
your absence.
The people who are always
not you.

I have been easy with trees
too long.
Too familiar with mountains.
Joy has been a habit.
Now
suddenly
this rain.

It was not impatience.
Impatient Orpheus was,
certainly, but no child.
And the provision was clear.
It was not impatience,
but despair. From the beginning,
it had gone badly.
From the beginning.
From the first laughter.
It was hell. Not a fable
of mechanical pain,
but the important made trivial.
Therefore the permission.
She had lived enough
in the always diversion.
Granted therefore.
It was not impatience,
but to have at least the face
seen freshly with loss
forever. A landscape.
It was not impatience.
He turned in despair.
And saw, at a distance, her back.

MALVOLIO IN SAN FRANCISCO

Two days ago they were playing the piano
with a hammer and blowtorch.
Next week they will read poetry
to saxophones.
And always they are building the Chinese Wall
of laughter.
They laugh so much.
So much more than I do.
And it doesn't wear them out
as it wears me out.
That's why your poetry's no good,
they say.
You should turn yourself upside down
so your ass would stick out,
they say.
And they seem to know.

They are right, of course.
I do feel awkward playing the game.
I do play the clown badly.
I cannot touch easily.
But I mistrust the ways of this city
with its white skies and weak trees.
One finds no impala here.
And the birds are pigeons.
The first-rate seems unknown
in this city of easy fame.
The hand's skill is always
from deliberate labor.

They put Phidias in prison
about his work on the Parthenon,

saying he had stolen gold.
And he probably had.
Those who didn't try to body Athena
they stayed free.

And Orpheus probably invited the rending
by his stubborn alien smell.
Poor Orpheus
who lost so much by making the difficult journey
when he might have grieved
easily.
Who tried to go back among the living
with the smell of journey on him.
Poor Orpheus
his stubborn tongue
blindly singing all the way to Lesbos.

What if I should go yellow-stockinged
and cross-gartered?
Suppose I did smile
fantastically,
kissed my hand to novelty,
what then?
Still would they imprison me in their dark house.
They would taunt me as doctors
concerned for my health
and laugh.
Always that consuming,
unrelenting laughter.

The musk deer is beguiled down from the great mountain
by flutes

to be fastened in a box
and tortured for the smell of his pain.

Yet somehow
there is somehow

I long for my old bigotry.

ORPHEUS IN GREENWICH VILLAGE

What if Orpheus,
confident in the hard-
found mastery,
should go down into Hell?
Out of the clean light down?
And then, surrounded
by the closing beasts
and readying his lyre,
should notice, suddenly,
they had no ears?

DON GIOVANNI ON HIS WAY TO HELL

The oxen have voices
the flowers are wounds
you never recover from Tuscany noons

    they cripple with beauty
    and butcher with love
    sing folly, sing flee, sing going down

the moon is corroding
the deer have gone lame
(but you never escape the incurably sane

    uncrippled by beauty
    unbutchered by love)
    sing folly, flee, sing going down

now it rains in your bowels
it rains though you weep
with terrible tameness it rains in your sleep

    and cripples with beauty
    and butchers with love

you never recover
you never escape
and you mustn't endeavor to find the mistake

    that cripples with beauty
    that butchers as love
    sing folly, sing flee, sing going down

    sing maidens and towns, oh maidens and towns
    folly, flee, sing going down

DON GIOVANNI ON HIS WAY TO HELL (II)

For Sue

How could they think women a recreation?
Or the repetition of bodies of steady interest?
Only the ignorant or the busy could. That elm
of flesh must prove a luxury of primes;
be perilous and dear with rain of an alternate earth.
Which is not to damn the forested China of touching.
I am neither priestly nor tired, and the great knowledge
of breasts with their loud nipples congregates in me.
The sudden nakedness, the small ribs, the mouth.
Splendid. Splendid. Splendid. Like Rome. Like loins.
A glamour sufficient to our long marvelous dying.
I say sufficient and speak with earned privilege,
for my life has been eaten in that foliate city.
To ambergris. But not for recreation.
I would not have lost so much for recreation.

Nor for love as the sweet pretend: the children's game
of deliberate ignorance of each to allow the dreaming.
Not for the impersonal belly nor the heart's drunkenness
have I come this far, stubborn, disastrous way.
But for relish of those archipelagoes of person.
To hold her in hand, closed as any sparrow,
and call and call forever till she turn from bird
to blowing woods. From woods to jungle. Persimmon.
To light. From light to princess. From princess to woman
in all her fresh particularity of difference.
Then oh, through the underwater time of night,
indecent and still, to speak to her without habit.
This I have done with my life, and am content.
I wish I could tell you how it is in that dark,
standing in the huge singing and the alien world.

BEFORE MORNING IN PERUGIA

Three days I sat
bewildered by love.
Three nights I watched
the gradations of dark.
Of light. Saw
three mornings begin,
and was taken each time
unguarded
of the loud bells.
My heart split open
as a melon.
And will not heal.
Gives itself
senselessly
to the old women
carrying milk.
The clumsy men sweeping.
To roofs.
God protect me.

MIDNIGHT IS MADE OF BRICKS

What pleasure hath it, to see in a mangled carcase?

—The Confessions of Saint Augustine

I am old of this ravening.
Poisoned of their God-damned flesh.
The ugly man-flesh.
And the fat woman-flesh.
I am tired and sick and old of it.
But the precise addiction is unrelenting.
Even now
it rouses sluggishly in me
and soon the imperious iron bells
bells
will begin
and the knowledge of the next one
will enter me
the realization of her walking peacefully
somehow toward our somewhere meeting.
The realization will come
and the need will be on me
and I must begin again.
Seeking along the great river of Fillmore
or the quiet river of Pacific Heights
with its birds.
Or through the cities of Market Street.
Perhaps this time it will be back
at the beginning
in North Beach.
In Vesuvio's maybe

where they come like deer.
Or The Place where they come like
ugly deer
laughing
and telling me
all intense
how they want to experience
everything.
Till the shouting begins in my head.
Asking me if I believe in Evil.
And the power climbs in me like Kong.

In the morning
it will be like every morning.
The filthy taste in my mouth
of old, clotting blood
the vomiting
and the murderous, stupid labor
with the stupid, open body.

THE NIGHT COMES EVERY DAY TO MY WINDOW

The night comes every day to my window.
The serious night, promising, as always,
age and moderation. And I am frightened
dutifully, as always, until I find
in the bed my three hearts and the cat
in my stomach talking, as always now,
of Gianna. And I am happy through the dark
with my feet singing of how she lies
warm and alone in her dark room
over Umbria where the brief and only
paradise flowers white by white.
I turn all night with the thought of her mouth
a little open, and hunger to walk
quiet in the Italy of her head, strange
but no tourist on the streets of her childhood.

MEELEE'S AWAY

(after Waley)

> Meelee's away in Lima.
> No one breeds flowers in my head.
> Of course, women do breed flowers in my head
>   but not like Meelee's—
>   So fragile, so pale.

THE ABNORMAL IS NOT COURAGE

The Poles rode out from Warsaw against the German
tanks on horses. Rode knowing, in sunlight, with sabers.
A magnitude of beauty that allows me no peace.
And yet this poem would lessen that day. Question
the bravery. Say it's not courage. Call it a passion.
Would say courage isn't that. Not at its best.
It was impossible, and with form. They rode in sunlight.
Were mangled. But I say courage is not the abnormal.
Not the marvelous act. Not Macbeth with fine speeches.
The worthless can manage in public, or for the moment.
It is too near the whore's heart: the bounty of impulse,
and the failure to sustain even small kindness.
Not the marvelous act, but the evident conclusion of being.
Not strangeness, but a leap forward of the same quality.
Accomplishment. The even loyalty. But fresh.
Not the Prodigal Son, nor Faustus. But Penelope.
The thing steady and clear. Then the crescendo.
The real form. The culmination. And the exceeding.
Not the surprise. The amazed understanding. The marriage,
not the month's rapture. Not the exception. The beauty
that is of many days. Steady and clear.
It is the normal excellence, of long accomplishment.

LIONS

I carried my house to Tijuana.
I carried my house through moonlight.
Through dirt streets of cribs
and faces clustered at dark windows.
Past soft voices and foolish calls
I carried my house.
To a bright room
with its nine girls,
the projector whirring,
and steady traffic to the wooden stalls.
Sleepy and sad,
I sat all night with the absurd young
listening to the true jungle in my house
where lions ate roses of blood
and sang of Alcibiades.

SUSANNA AND THE ELDERS

It is foolish for Rubens to show her
simpering. They were clearly guilty
and did her much sorrow. But this poem
is not concerned with justice.
It concerns itself with fear.
If it could, it would force you to see
them at the hedge with their feeble eyes,
the bodies, and the stinking mouths.
To see the one with the trembling hands.
The one with the sun visor.
It would show through the leaves
all the loveliness of the world
compacted. The lavish gleaming.
Her texture. The sheen of water on her
brightness. The moon in sunlight.
Not only the choir of flesh.
Nor the intimacy of her inner mouth.
A meadow of warmth inhabited.
Personal. And the elders excluded
forever. Forever in exile.
It would show you their inexact hands
till you acknowledged how it comes on you.

I think of them pushing to the middle
of Hell where the pain is strongest.
To see at the top of the chimney,
far off, the small coin of color.
And, sometimes, leaves.

THE FOUR PERFECTLY TANGERINES

The four perfectly tangerines were a
clue
as they sat
singing
(three to one)
in that ten-thirty
a.m. room
not unhappily of death
singing of how they were tangerines
against white
but how
against continuous orange
they were only
fruit.

One sang of God
of his eight thousand green faces
and the immediate glory of his
pavilioned
dancing.

Three sang of how you can't go back.

One sang of the seeds in his heart
of how
inside the tangerine-colored skin
inside his flesh
(which was the color of
tangerines)
were little
seeds
which were

inside
green.

So
I opened the one
and the odor of his breaking
was the sweet breasts
of being no longer
only.

THE FIRST MORNING OF THE WORLD ON LONG ISLAND

For Doris

The provisional and awkward harp
of me
makes nothing of you now.
I labor to constrain it
but am unschooled and cannot.
One learns to play the harp,
said Aristotle, by playing.
But I do not. Such a harp
grows always more dear
and I manage always less truly
well. Each visitor offhand
does better. While I with this year
of loss can do nothing.
Can say nothing of the smell
of rain in the desert
and the cottonwoods blowing
above us. If it would tell
even so little of Council Bluffs.
But it will not.
I can make it mourn
but not celebrate the River
nor my happiness in having been
of you.

I'LL TRY TO EXPLAIN ABOUT THE FEAR

I'll try to explain about the fear
again
since you think my trouble with the whales
and elephants is a question of size.
I'm on the other inhabited island
of the Tremiti group,
looking across evening on the water
and up the enormous cliffs
to San Nicola.
I've been watching the few weak lights
begin,
thinking of Alcibiades
and those last years at Trebizond.
I've been looking at San Nicola
huddled behind the great, ruined
fortifications,
and thinking how the dark is leaking
out of the broken windows.
How the doors on those stone houses
are banging and banging and banging.
I've been remembering the high grass
in the piazza.
And Rimbaud in the meaningless jungle.
I know the business of the whales
may bring me there.
That trying to understand about the elephants,
about my stunned heart,
may require it.
May choose that for the last years.
A bare white room
overlooking the cathedral.
High up there
with the pure light
and the lust.

POEM FOR LAURA

Now come the bright prophets across my life.
The solemn flesh, the miracles, and the pain.
Across the simple meadows of my heart,
splendidly you come promising sorrow.
And knowing, I bless your coming with trees of love,
singing, singing even to the night.

The princely mornings will fail when you go, and night
will come like animals. Yet I open my cautious life
and sing thanksgiving of yes, oh yes to love,
even while the tireless crows of pain
and the diligent fever-ticks of sorrow
are somehow privileged in my flowering heart.

For you fashion such rivers in my soon unable heart
as are focused to paradise by the crippling night.
Such terraced waters as are cheap at only sorrow.
And to have cargoes of hyacinths sail once more my life
I will freely undertake any debt of pain.
I will break these hands for tokens, oh my love.

NEW YORK, SUMMER

I'd walk her home after work,
buying roses and talking of Bechsteins.
She was full of soul.
Her small room was gorged with heat,
and there were no windows.
She'd take off everything
but her pants,
and take the pins from her hair,
throwing them on the floor
with a great noise.
Like Crete.
We wouldn't make love.
She'd get on the bed
with those nipples,
and we'd lie
sweating
and talking of my best friend.
They were in love.
When I got quiet,
she'd put on usually Debussy,
and,
leaning down to the small ribs,
bite me.
Hard.

THE BAY BRIDGE FROM POTRERO HILL

Pure
every day there's the bridge
every day there's the bridge
every day there's the bridge
every day there's the bridge
and each night.
It's not easy to live this way.

Once
the bridge was small and stone-white
and called the Pont au Change
or the Pont Louis-Philippe.
We went home at midnight
to the Île Saint-Louis as deer
through a rustle of bells.
Six years distant
and the Atlantic
and a continent.
The way I was then
and the way I am now.
A long time.

I fed in the bright parts of the forest,
stinting to pass among the impala.
But one can acquire a taste for love
as for loneliness
or ugliness
as for saintliness.
Each a special way of going down.

That was a sweet country
and large.
Ample with esplanades,

easy with apricots.
A happy country.
But a country for children.

Now
every day there's the bridge.
Every day there's the exacting,
literal, foreign country of the heart.
Toads and panders
ruined horses
pears
terrifying honey
heralds
heralds

ON GROWING OLD IN SAN FRANCISCO

Two girls barefoot walking in the rain
both girls lovely, one of them is sane
hurting me softly
hurting me though
two girls barefoot walking in the snow
walking in the white snow
walking in the black
two girls barefoot never coming back

WITHOUT WATTEAU, WITHOUT BURCKHARDT, OKLAHOMA

In April, holding my house and held
unprepared in the stomach of death,
I receive the vacant landscape of America.

In April, before the concealment of beauty,
the vacant landscape of America, bright,
comes through me. Comes through my house like Laura.

Intractable, the states of reality come,
lordly, in April, Texas, impossibly
to this house furnished with the standard half-

consummated loves: Vienna under rain,
summer in the mountains above Como, Provence
the special country of my heart. In April,

inadvertently, at thirty-three, filled
with walled towns of lemon trees, I am
unexpectedly alone in West Virginia.

LETTER TO MR. JOHN KEATS

The Spanish Steps—February 23, 1961

What can I do with these people?
They come to the risk so dutifully.
Are delighted by anecdotes that give
them Poetry. Are grateful to be told
of diagonals that give them Painting.
Good people. But stubborn when warned
the beast is not domestic.

How can I persuade them
that the dark, soulful Keats
was five feet one?
Liked fighting and bear-baiting?
I can't explain the red hair.
Nor say how you died so full
of lust for Fanny Brawne.

I will tell them of Semele.

PORTOLANO

"Asti kasmin-cit pradese nagaram"

In your thin body is an East of wonder.
In your walking are accounts of morning.
Your hands are legends, and your mouth a proof of kilins.
    But the way is long
    and the roads bad.

Beyond the crucial pass of Tauris
past the special lure of vice
beyond Persepolis and the ease of Badakhshan
stretches a waste of caution.
    The route is difficult
    and the maps wrong.

If one survives the singing-sands of pride
and the always drumming hill of fear
he finds an impregnable range of moderation.
    Ascent is dangerous
    and the cold maims.

Could one get through, the brilliance of Cambaluc
and the wealth of Shangtu would be there, no doubt;
but what of the Bamboo Pavilion? It is fashioned, they say,
to be easily dismantled and moved.
    The Khan is seventy
    and the Ming strong.

In your thin body is an East of wander.
In your seeking are distraints of mourning.

While Venice is close at hand—to be taken now or lost.
  The season of grace
  may be spent once.

In the pavilion, they say, are birds.

IT IS CLEAR WHY THE ANGELS COME NO MORE

It is clear why the angels come no more.
Standing so large in their beautiful Latin,
how could they accept being refracted
so small in another grammar, or leave
their perfect singing for this broken speech?
Why should they stumble this alien world?

Always I have envied the angels their grace.
But I left my hope of Byzantine size
and came to this awkwardness, this stupidity.
Came finally to you washing my face
as everyone laughed, and found a forest
opening as marriage ran in me. All

the leaves in the world turned a little
singing: the angels are wrong.

THE WHITENESS, THE SOUND, AND ALCIBIADES

So I come on this birthday at last
here in the house of strangers.
With a broken pair of shoes,
no profession, and a few poems.
After all that promise.
Not by addiction or play, by choices.
By concern for whales and love,
for elephants and Alcibiades.
But to arrive at so little product.
A few corners done,
an arcade up but unfaced,
and everywhere the ambitious
unfinished monuments to Myshkin
and magnitude. Like persisting
on the arrogant steeple of Beauvais.

I wake in Trastevere
in the house of city-peasants,
and lie in the noise dreaming
on the wealth of summer nights
from my childhood when the dark
was sixty feet deep in luxury,
of elm and maple and sycamore.
I wandered hour by hour
with my gentle, bewildered need,
following the faint sound
of women in the moving leaves.

In Latium, years ago,
I sat by the road watching

an ox come through the day.
Stark-white in the distance.
Occasionally under a tree.
Colorless in the heavy sun.
Suave in the bright shadows.
Starch-white near in the glare.
Petal-white near in the shade.
Linen, stone-white, and milk.
Ox-white before me, and past
into the thunder of light.

For ten years I have tried
to understand about the ox.
About the sound. The whales.
Of love. And arrived here
to give thanks for the profit.
I wake to the wanton freshness.
To the arriving and leaving. To the journey.
I wake to the freshness. And do reverence.

MONOLITHOS:

Poems 1962 and 1982

[1982]

Monolithos *means* single stone, *and refers to the small
hill behind our house which gave the place we lived its
name. It is the tip of a non-igneous stone island buried
in debris when most of Thíra blew apart 3,500 years ago.*

—J.G.

ONE — 1962

BETWEEN POEMS

A lady asked me
what poets do
between poems.
Between passions
and visions. I said
that between poems
I provided for death.
She meant as to jobs
and commonly.
Commonly, I provide
against my death,
which comes on.
And give thanks
for the women I have
been privileged to
in extreme.

THE PLUNDERING OF CIRCE

Circe had no pleasure in pigs.
Pigs, wolves, nor fawning
lions. She sang in our language
and, beautiful, waited for quality.

Every month they came
struggling up from the cove.
The great sea-light behind them.
Each time maybe a world.

Season after season.
Dinner after dinner.
And always at the first measures
of lust became themselves.

Odysseus? A known liar.
A resort darling. Untouchable.

ISLANDS AND FIGS

The sky
on and on,
stone.
The Mediterranean
down the cliff,
stone.
These fields,
rock.
Dead weeds
everywhere.
And the weight
of sun.
In the weeds
an old woman
lifting off
snails.
Near
two trees
of ripe figs.
The heart
never fits
the journey.
Always
one ends
first.

POETRY IS A KIND OF LYING

Poetry is a kind of lying,
necessarily. To profit the poet
or beauty. But also in
that truth may be told only so.

Those who, admirably, refuse
to falsify (as those who will not
risk pretensions) are excluded
from saying even so much.

Degas said he didn't paint
what he saw, but what
would enable them to see
the thing he had.

FOR EXAMPLE

For example, that fragment of entablature
in the Museo delle Terme. It continues
giant forever. Without seasons.
Ambergris of the Latin whale.
For years he dealt with it, month by month
in his white room above Perugia
while thousands of swifts turned
in the structures of sun with a sound like glass.
Strained to accommodate it
in the empty streets of Rome. Singing
according to whether bells preempted the dark
or rain ordered the earth. And even now,
like Kurtz, he crawls toward the lethal merit.

THE SIRENS AGAIN

What are we to do about loveliness? We get past
that singing early and reach an honest severity.
We all were part of the Children's Crusade: trusted,
were sold bad boats, and went under. But we still
dream of the voices. Not to go back. Thinking
to go on even into the confusion of pleasure.
We hear them carol at night and do not mind the lies,
intending to come on those women from inland.

ALBA

After a summer with happy people,
I rush back, scared, gulping
down pain wherever I can get it.

OSTINATO RIGORE

As slowly as possible, I said,
and we went into paradise.
Rushes alternate with floating islands
of tomatoes. Stretches of lily pads
and then lotus. The kingfishers
flash and go into the lake,
making a sound in the silence.
After, I can hear her breathing.
The Japanese built gardens eight
hundred years ago as a picture
of the Pure Land, because people
could not imagine a happy life.
My friend lives on the Delaware River
and fashions Eden out of burned
buildings that were the Automats
of his youth in New York.
Another designs a country
with justice for everyone.
I know a woman who makes heaven
out of her body. I lie in the smell
of water, with the sun going down,
trying to figure out this painful
model I have carpentered together.

A BIRD SINGS TO ESTABLISH FRONTIERS

Perhaps if we could begin some definite way.
At a country inn of the old Russian novels,
maybe. A contrived place to establish manner.
With roles of traditional limit for distance.
I might be going back, and there would be a pause.
Late at night, while they changed the horses on your sled.
Or prepared my room. An occasion to begin.
Though not on false terms. I am not looking for love.
I have what I can manage, and too many claims.
Just a formal conversation, with no future.
But I must explain that I will probably cry.
It is important you ignore it. I am fine.
I am not interested in discussing it.
It is complicated and not amiable.
The sort of thing our arrangements provide against.
There should be a fireplace. Brandy, and some cigars.
Or cheese with warm crackers. Anything that permits
the exercise of incidental decorum:
deferring to the other's preceding, asking
for a light. Vintages. It does not matter what.
The fireplace is to allow a different grace.
And there will be darkness above new snow outside.
Even if we agree on a late afternoon,
there would still be snow. Inside, the dining room must
have a desolate quality. So we can talk
without raising our voices. Finally, I hope
it is understood we are not to meet again.
And that both of us are men, so all that other
is avoided. We can speak and preserve borders.
The tears are nothing. The real sorrow is for that
old dream of nobility. All those gentlemen.

BARTLEBY AT THE WALL

The wall
is the side of a building.
Maybe seventy-five feet high.
The rope is tied
below the top
and hangs down thirty feet.
Just hangs down.
Above the slum lot.
It's been there a long time.
One part
below the middle
is frayed.
I've been at this all month.
Trying to see the rope.
The wall.
Carefully looking
at the bricks.
Seeing they are
umber and soot
and the color of tongue.
Even counting them.
But it's like Poussin.
Too clear.
The way things aren't.
So I try not staring.
Not grabbing.
Allowing it to come.
But just at the point
where I'd see,
the mind gives a little
skip

and I'm already past.
To all this sorrow again.
Considering
the skip between wildness
and affection,
where everything is.

TWO — [MONOLITHOS] — 1982

ALL THE WAY FROM THERE TO HERE

From my hill I look down on the freeway and over
to a gull lifting black against the gray ridge.
It lifts slowly higher and enters the bright sky.
Surely our long, steady dying brings us to a state
of grace. What else can I call this bafflement?

From here I deal with my irrelevance to love.
With the bewildering tenderness of which I am
composed. The sun goes down and comes up again.
The moon comes up and goes down. I live
with the morning air and the different airs of night.
I begin to grow old.

The ships put out and are lost.
Put out and are lost.
Leaving me with their haunting awkwardness
and the imperfection of birds. While all the time
I work to understand this happiness I have come into.

What I remember of my nine-story fall
down through the great fir is the rush of green.
And the softness of my regret in the ambulance going
to my nearby death, looking out at the trees leaving me.

What I remember of my crushed spine
is seeing Linda faint again and again,
sliding down the white X-ray room wall
as my sweet body flailed on the steel table
unable to manage the bulk of pain. That
and waiting in the years after for the burning
in my fingertips, which would announce,
the doctors said, the beginning of paralysis.

What I remember best of the four years of watching
in Greece and Denmark and London and Greece is Linda
making lunch. Her blondeness and ivory coming up
out of the blue Aegean. Linda walking with me daily
across the island from Monolithos to Thíra and back.
That's what I remember most of death:
the gentleness of us in that bare Greek Eden,
the beauty as the marriage steadily failed.

NOT PART OF LITERATURE

Monolithos was four fisherman huts along the water,
a miniature villa closed for years, and our farmhouse
a hundred feet behind. Hot fields of barley, grapes,
and tomatoes stretching away three flat miles
to where the rest of the island used to be.
Where the few people live above the great cliffs.
A low mountain to the south and beyond that the earth
filled with pictures of Atlantis. On our wrong side
of the island were no people, cars, plumbing, or lights.
The summer skies and Mediterranean constantly. No trees.
Me cleaning squid. Linda getting up from a chair.

TRYING TO BE MARRIED

Watching my wife out in the full moon,
the sea bright behind her across the field
and through the trees. Eight years
and her love for me quieted away.
How fine she is. How hard we struggle.

REGISTRATION

Where the worms had opened the owl's chest,
he could see, inside her frail ribs,
the city of Byzantium. Exquisitely made
of ironwood and brass. The pear trees around
the harem and the warships were perfectly detailed.
No wonder they make that mewing sound, he thought,
calling to each other among the dark arbors
while the cocks crow and answer and a farther
rooster answers that: the sound proceeding
up the mountain, paling and thinning until
it is transparent, like the faint baying of hounds.

MORE THAN FRIENDS

I was walking through the harvested fields
tonight and got thinking about age.
Began wondering if my balance was gone.
So there I was out in the starlight
on one foot, swaying, and cheating.

THAT TENOR OF WHICH THE NIGHT BIRDS
ARE A VEHICLE

The great light within the blackness shines out
as the cry of owls and tranced signaling of nightjars.
Birds who are vast cloud-chambers of the place I am
in my bright condition, a neighborhood I am the darkness of.
It should come from me as song and new flying
between the pale olive trees. But the calling of birds
in the silent dim fields is a translation I fail at,
despite the steady gladness where I have made landfall.
I go without audible music, flying heavily
from stone to stone in order to nest in marble.
Failing the harking, missing the hawking. Not managing
as a bird. Struggling through my career, blindly testing
the odor of all that whiteness night after night:
not sure if the old piss-smell is the scent of gods,
and knowing even that faint clue is fading as I hesitate.

WALKING HOME ACROSS THE ISLAND

Walking home across the plain in the dark.
And Linda crying. Again we have come
to a place where I rail and she suffers and the moon
does not rise. We have only each other,
but I am shouting inside the rain
and she is crying like a wounded animal,
knowing there is no place to turn. It is hard
to understand how we could be brought here by love.

MISTRUST OF BRONZE

The sun is perfect, but it makes no nightingales sing.
The violence of light suppresses color in these fields,
its glare masking the green of the white grapes
and masking the heavy purple. Just as the moon now
finds no tinge in the giant oleander. Perhaps it is
bronze models for the spirit that endanger us.

I think of my years on the Greyhound bus, living with
the blank earth under the American sun day after day.
Leaking away into those distances. Waxing again
in the night while everyone slept and I watched
the old snow by the fences just after the headlights.
I used to blur in the dark thinking of the long counter
at Rock Springs day after tomorrow, my pleasure
of hunger merging with the bad food.
Memories make me grainy and distinct somewhere. Where
night shudders with a black fire of which Dante tells.

I begin the long inaccuracy alone.
Loneliness, they report, is a man's fate.
A man's fate, said Heraclitus, is his character.
I sit masturbating in the moonlight,
trying to find means for all of it.
The sea collapses, again and again, faintly behind me.
I walk down the dirt road, touch the cold Aegean,
and come back slowly. My hand drying in the night air.

ANGELUS

Obsidian. Sturgeon. Infatuated angels.
Which only we can translate into flesh.
The language to which we alone are native.
Our own bait. We are spirits housed in meat,
instantly opaque to the Lord. As Jesus.
We go into the deadfall of the body,
our hearts in their marvelous cases,
and discover new belfries everywhere.

I continued toward the Minotaur to keep
the thread taut. And suddenly, now,
immense flowers are coloring all
my stalked body. Making wine of me.
As bells get music of metal in the rain.
The prey I am willingly prospers.
The exile that comes on comes too late.
I go to it as Adam, singing across paradise.

A KIND OF WORLD

Things that are themselves. Waves water, the rocks
stone. The smell of her arms. Stillness. Windstorms.
The long silence again. The well. The rabbit. Heat.
Nipples and long thighs. Her heavy bright mane.
Plunging water flashing as she washes her body in the sun.
"Perfect in whiteness." Light going away every evening
like some great importance. Grapes outside the windows.
Linda talking less and less. Going down to the sea
while she sleeps. Standing in the cold water to my mouth
just before morning. Linda saying late in the day
we should eat now or it would be too dark to wash the dishes.
She going out quietly afterward to scream into the wind
from the ocean. Coming in. Lighting the lamps.

LEAVING MONOLITHOS

They were cutting the spring barley by fistfuls
when we came. Boys drove horses and mules over it
all day in threshing pits under the powerful sky.
They came from their white village on the horizon
for tomatoes in June. And later for grapes.
Now they are plowing in the cold wind. Yesterday
I burned my papers by the wall. This morning I look
back at the lone, shuttered farmhouse. Sun rising
over the volcano. At the full moon above the sea.

DIVORCE

Woke up suddenly thinking I heard crying.
Rushed through the dark house.
Stopped, remembering. Stood looking
out at the bright moonlight on concrete.

REMEMBERING MY WIFE

I see them in black and white as they wait,
severely happy, in the sunlight of Thermopylae.
As Iseult and Beatrice are always black and white.
I imagine Helen in light, not hue. In my dreams,
Nausicaä is blanched colorless by noon.
And Botticelli's Simonetta comes as faint tints of air.
Cleopatra is in color almost to the end.
Like Linda's blondeness dyed by flowers and the sea.
I loved that wash of color, but remember her
mostly black and white. Mark Antony listening
to Hercules abandoning him listened in the dark.
In that finer time of day. In the essence, not the mode.

PEWTER

Thrushes flying under the lake. Nightingales singing underground.
Yes, my King. Paris hungry and leisurely just after the war. Yes.
America falling into history. Yes. Those silent winter afternoons
along the Seine when I was always alone. Yes, my King. Rain
everywhere in the forests of Pennsylvania as the king's coach
lumbered and was caught and all stood gathered close
while the black trees went on and on. Ah, my King,
it was the sweet time of our lives: the rain shining on their faces,
the loud sound of rain around. Like the nights we waited,
knowing she was probably warm and moaning under someone else.
That cold mansard looked out over the huge hospital of the poor
and far down on Paris, gray and beautiful under the February rain.
Between that and this. That yes and this yes. Between, my King,
that forgotten girl, forgotten pain, and the consequence.
Those lovely, long-ago night bells that I did not notice grow
more and more apparent in me. Like pewter expanding as it cools.
Yes, like a king halted in the great forest of Pennsylvania.
Like me singing these prison songs to praise the gray,
to praise her, to tell of me, yes, and of you, my King.

He struggles to get the marble terrace clear
in his dreams. Broad steps going down.
A balustrade cut into the bright moonlight.
Love is pouring out and he is crying.
All the romantic equipment. But it is not that.
He looks down on the gray night in the black pool.
Sculpture glimmers in the weeds around it.
Why is the small-headed Artemis so moving,
and the Virtues with their pretty breasts?
He is not foolish. He knows better.
The scuffing of his shoes on the stairs is loud.
What is he searching for among the banal statues?
When he touches the chapped plinths, his spirit twangs.
Derision protects him less and less. He goes
shamelessly among them, trembling, fashioning a place.

HUNGER

Digging into the apple
with my thumbs.
Scraping out the clogged nails
and digging deeper.
Refusing the moon color.
Refusing the smell and memories.
Digging in with the sweet juice
running along my hands unpleasantly.
Refusing the sweetness.
Turning my hands to gouge out chunks.
Feeling the juice sticky
on my wrists. The skin itching.
Getting to the wooden part.
Getting to the seeds.
Going on.
Not taking anyone's word for it.
Getting beyond the seeds.

SECTS

We were talking about tent revivals
and softshell Baptists and the one-suspender Amish
and being told whistling on Sunday made the Madonna cry.
One fellow said he was raised in a church that taught
wearing yellow and black together was an important sin.
It got me thinking of the failed denomination
I was part of: that old false dream of woman.
I believed it was a triumph to have access to their mystery.
To see the hidden hair, to feel my spirit topple over,
to lie together in the afternoon while it rained
all the way to Indonesia. I had crazy ideas of what it was.
Like being in a dark woods at night
when an invisible figure crosses the stiff snow,
making a sound like some other planet's machinery.

THEY CALL IT ATTEMPTED SUICIDE

My brother's girlfriend was not prepared for how much blood
splashed out. He got home in time, but was angry
about the mess she had made of his room. I stood behind,
watching them turn it into something manageable. Thinking
how frightening it must have been before things had names.
We say *peony* and make a flower out of that slow writhing.
Deal with the horror of recurrence by calling it
a million years. The death everywhere is no trouble
once you see it as nature, landscape, or botany.

MENISCUS

The French woman says, Stop, you're breaking my dress.
She tells him she must meet her friends in the Plaka.
His heels click back and forth. Stop that,
she says, you know I don't like being hit.
More bickering and hitting and then her shutter
closes. Fifteen minutes later, the light goes on
and they are lovers. They speak to each other
in ordinary voices as I watch the moon rise.

WHO'S THERE

I hear the trees with surprise after California,
having forgotten the sound that filled my childhood.
I hear the maples and vast elms again. American oak,
English oak, pin oak. Honey locust and mountain ash.
Catalpa, beech, and sycamore. I hear the luxury again
just before autumn. And remember the old riddle:
Winter will take it all, the trees will go on.
This grass will die and this lawn continue. What then
goes on of the child I was? Of that boy taunted
by the lush whispering every summer night in Pittsburgh?
All those I have been are the generalization that tastes
this plum. Brothers who knew all the women I loved.
But did we share or alternate? Was I with Gianna
among the olive trees those evenings in Perugia?
Am I the one who heard with Linda the old Danish men
singing up out of the snow and dark far down below us?

MEANING WELL

Marrying is like somebody
throwing the baby up.
It happy and them throwing it
higher. To the ceiling.
Which jars the loose bulb
and it goes out
as the baby starts down.

TEMPLATE

Our slow crop is used up within an hour. So I live
effortlessly by the ocean, where the sun bestows
and bestows and I return nothing. Go cross-grain through
the fire and call my style lust. But the night forces me.
I get so quiet lying under the stars I can't regulate
the sound of owls altering me. In that dark in front
of the house, I often think of an old man at Sadler's Wells.
The only one left who had seen the famous dances.
When they did them again, despite the bad notation,
he would watch patiently, saying, No, no, that's not the way
it was somehow. Until they got it right. But he died.

SIEGE

We think there is a sweetness concealed in the rain,
a presence in the ebullient wet thicket.
And we are wrong.
Summer, the rain, oh Lord, the rain
hammers us into a joy,
which we call divinity.
And we are mistaken.
The heart's weather of nipple and music
condenses only on the soft metal of personal knowledge.
Our presence is the savor.
We must get to the iron valve in the center
of that meaningless leafage.
Going past even the statuary and the unnaturalness
our faith is founded on.
To close it down.
To reduce that earthquake of flux.
Reducing it to human use.

TRANSLATION INTO THE ORIGINAL

Apollo walks the deep roads back in the hills
through sleet to the warm place she is.
Eats her fine cunt and afterward they pretend
to watch the late movie to cover their happiness.
He swims with his body in the empty Tyrrhenian Sea.
Comes out of that summer purple with his mind.
Cherishes and makes all year in the city.
But Apollo is not reasonable about desire.
This wolf god, rust god, lord of the countryside.
God of dance and lover of mortal women. Homer said he
is fierce. His coming like the swift coming of night.
That the gods feel fear and awe in the presence
of this lawgiver, explainer of the rules of death.
Averter of evil and praiser of the best.
The violent indifference of Dionysus makes nothing
live. Awful Apollo stands in the brilliant fields,
watching the wind change the olive trees.
He comes back through the dark singing
so quietly that you can hear nothing.

BURNING AND FATHERING: ACCOUNTS OF MY COUNTRY

The classical engine of death moves my day. Hurrying me.
Harrowing. Tempering everything piece by piece
in a mighty love of perfection, and leaving each part
broken in turn. I walk through the energy of this slum,
walking there by the Loire among the châteaux of my country.
"Banquets where beautiful and virtuous ladies walked
half-naked, with their hair loose like brides." Or François
Premier blossoming in that first spring of France.
                                                    Flickering.
As Diane de Poitiers flickers. As the ladies of Watteau flicker.
As these fine houses blur to tenements. Beyond, in the park,
the great eucalyptus are clearly provisional, waning in time.
And there are gods in the palace of leaves, their faint glaze
showing briefly as they promenade in the high air, going away.
François Premier dimming. The trees shuddering. The gods,
the Loire, flickering at night. My country, which does not exist,
failing. I walk here singing there by the river with all times
and places flickering and singing about me in their dialects
as I go back into the slum dreaming of Helen washing her breasts
in the Turkish morning.
                        But she wavers and cracks. Suddenly
the towers go down everywhere. Everything is breaking.
Everything is lost in the fire and lost in the gauging. Fire
burning inside of fire, where love celebrates but cannot preserve.
The marble heart of the world fractures. The unrelenting engine

tests everything with a steel exigence, and returns it maimed.
And yet all we have is somehow born in that murdering.
Born in the fire and born in the breaking. Something is perfected.
François Premier changes as he watches the dying Leonardo drag
through the splendid corridors. Pressure of that terrible intolerance
gets brandy in the welter. Such honey of that heavy rider.

THE FASHIONABLE HEART

The Chinese, to whom the eighteenth-century English
sent for their elaborate sets of dishes,
followed the accompanying designs faithfully:
writing red in the spaces where it said red,
yellow where it said yellow.

BREAKFAST

It was a fine Leghorn egg,
and inside, unexpectedly, was the city
of Byzantium. Even from that height
he could see the flash of bedding
at the windows, the lump of Hagia Sophia,
and blue flags on the enormous city walls.
Clearly it was midsummer. Right,
he thought, remembering about love.
Not wanting the responsibility.
Watching the flies begin at it.

LOSING

I worked my way up the terraced gardens behind the house
and around to the side. Until I could see into the library.
They were all there except Walter. It would have to do.
I regretted the rain. It made me emotional.
Anna had put a coat around her instead of dressing again.
The men were gathered around the children.
She was over by their mother looking at his Corot.
I set up the detonator. There was still six minutes.
It might be too long. Already memories were leaking in.
How poor I was that year in Deauville. And how young.
I thought of the Hôtel du Nord, and of the bar down the block
where I used to meet her. (The rain and the smell of night
pulled at me. Confused me.) Everything means a choice,
she had said, getting one thing and losing one. The love still
held me, but all at once I could, despite the rain, admit
to myself what I really wanted was this clarity.

THE RAINY FORESTS OF NORTHERN CALIFORNIA

The fellow came back to rape her again last night,
but this time her former husband was there.
Why did you rape her, you son of a bitch? he said.
I didn't, he answered, she let me.
Sure, because you hit her, that's why she let you.
And it dwindled away into definitions.

IL MIO TESORO

Most nights he would be upstairs with the wife
while his friend in the living room played
the same aria again and again, the pain
flowing over their wet, happy bodies.

DON GIOVANNI IN TROUBLE

The orchard changed. His appetite drifted.
In the bedrooms, on the ships, under bushes.
He was distracted by the miscellany
of their dressing tables, or the blonde's
small scar just as she began to yield.
The contessa caught him looking past the nipples
to her unusual toes. He hurried on,
but she stayed uneasy. As he was.
Still loving it, but thinking of the Lipizzaners:
wondering what those horses were like before
they became a beautiful performance.

THE MOVIES

He realized that night how much he was in their power.
Ludwig was insolent from the time he arrived
and insisted the projection should be on a plum.
The purple made a poor screen, and at that distance
it was impossible to get any sort of real focus.
He could see the phosphorescence of her body
in the stamp of light, but not her expression
as she turned from kissing the Japanese. The man and bed
drifted smaller and smaller as she came forward.
He could feel his heart as he strained to see.
She showed herself, as usual, naked except for
the black stockings he sent last time. She continued
toward the camera until the screen was an even white.
He sat there in the kitchen thinking it had gone on
so long now these people were the only family he had.

BYZANTIUM BURNING

When I looked at the stubborn dark Buddha
high in the forest, I noticed crimson
just along where his lips closed.
And understood Byzantium was burning.
So there would be no more injustice.
Unless everyone can sit on a throne
that rises and has enameled birds that sing,
no one should sit on such a throne.
Such a city measures the merit of villagers.
So it was all perishing in there at last.
The definitions of space by basilicas.
The shape of law in the mind of Justinian.
But how could he dare, this opulent Buddha
with his temples and everyone adoring,
preach to me of the ordinary? Who was he
to subtract Byzantium from the size of my people?
So I begin to sing. Build and sing.
Sing and build inside my thin lips.

THEY WILL PUT MY BODY INTO THE GROUND

They will put my body into the ground.
Chemistry will have its way for a time,
and then large beetles will come.
After that, the small beetles. Then
the disassembling. After that, the Puccini
will dwindle the way light goes
from the sea. Even Pittsburgh will
vanish, leaving a greed tough as winter.

LOVE POEM

The couple on the San Francisco bus looked Russian,
and spoke what sounded like it. He was already an old man
at fifty. She could have been his wife or daughter.
At first I thought she was retarded. She was probably drunk
and maybe stupid. He had on a gray suit and was always angry.
Whatever she did made him glare and tug at her sleeve.
She fought back dutifully, but without conviction.
Knowing her role was to be wrong. She was wrong. She had
the whole bus watching. It was hard to quarrel properly,
also because everything pleased her so much.
She craned to read the advertisements
or twisted around to see out the other window
or stared with her mouth open at the people who got on.
When there was a seat they could sit in together,
she messed it up. He went to the rear.
She kept whispering, and signaling who would get off next.
He sat proud and closed on a seat that ran the wrong way,
getting thrown about. She wore a cheap babushka
and a foolish old coat and white socks.
Even stopping for red lights pleased her.
Finally a place was empty and she plunged into it,
crying to him and making great scooping gestures.
He pretended not to hear. But she just got louder in her delight,
until she was standing, guarding the seat, and calling
the length of the bus. He had no choice.
She settled in as happy as anyone I ever saw,
pointing out the ads for him all over again.

ELEPHANT HUNT IN GUADALAJARA

El Serape's floor show finished at one. The lights
went off and strong girls came like tin moths.
To dance carefully with us for eight cents.
Now at last the old tenor has begun the deadly
three o'clock show with its granite Mexican music.
The girls are asleep in the side booths.
Where is it? Where in the name of Christ is it?

PAVANE

I thought it said on the girl's red purse
A kind of sad dance and all day
wondered what was being defined.
Wisdom? The history of Poland?
All the ways of growing old?
No, I decided (walking back
to the hotel this morning), it must be love.
The real love that follows
early delight and ignorance.
A wonderful sad dance that comes after.

LOYALTY

About once a month the beautiful girl
who was my wife or one of our friends
comes to say how they defended me
when the others said I was growing old.

SONG

Rotting herds everywhere on the outskirts.
And the old man shuffling among the carrion
with his dim flashlight. Not trusting his memory.
Practicing over and over so that when the time comes
he will automatically say no. Salvaging at least that.

GETTING READY

What if the heart does not pale as the body wanes,
but is like the sun that blazes hotter each day
on these immense, perishing fields? What then?
(Desire is not the problem. This far south,
we are careful not to mistake seizures for love.)
He sits there bewildered in a clamp of light.
In the stillness, the sun grinds him clean.

SUL PONTICELLO

Year by year he works himself,
replacing youth with stone.
But the marble rings with love
even more than the fine flesh.

THE CUCUMBERS OF PRAXILLA OF SICYON

What is the best we leave behind?
Certainly love and form and ourselves.
Surely those. But it is the mornings
that are hard to relinquish, and music
and cucumbers. Rain on trees, empty
piazzas in small towns flooded with sun.
What we are busy with doesn't make us
groan *ah! ah!* as we will for the nights
and the cucumbers.

A DESCRIPTION OF HAPPINESS IN KØBENHAVN

All this windless day snow fell
into the King's Garden
where I walked, perfecting and growing old,
abandoning one by one everybody:
randomly in love with the paradise
furnace of my mind. Now I sit in the dark,
dreaming of a marble sun
and its strictness. This
is to tell you I am not coming back.
To tell you instead of my private life
among people who must wrestle their hearts
in order to feel anything, as though it were
unnatural. What I master by day
still lapses in the night. But I go on
with the cargo cult, blindly feeling the snow
come down, learning to flower by tightening.

NEW HAMPSHIRE MARBLE

I called Sue the week I moved back from Rome.
She was getting married on Sunday she said,
but would drive over after lunch to say goodbye.
Later, in the tall grass between some homes,
we were searching around in the torn dirt,
frantic and laughing. Trying to find
the huge diamond engagement ring.
Our bodies flaring in the winter moonlight.

MY MARRIAGE WITH MRS. JOHNSON

When the storm hit, I was fording the river
and thinking of Doctor Johnson. Garrick, as a boy,
spied on that bulbous man doting on his blowsy wife.
For years did the famous imitation for London society
of those walruses pretending to be lovers. I was
thinking of Johnson's permanent sadness after she died.
I looked up at the palms floundering in the warm rain
and out at the waves piling up in the cove.
I thought of the foolish earth and how we dally
in my bed. The absurd exaggeration of her.
She lies with me after singing, singing, singing,
singing—Oh, it is such a marriage, however it looks
through any keyhole. I went on, carrying the fish,
feeling for the bottom, and dreaming of us entering
the great hall at Versailles: everyone gaping
and elaborate Louis Quatorze wondering at his envy.

HEART SKIDDING

The pigeon with a broken wing.
The pigeon with no left foot.
That pigeon with his beak grown wrong
starving among the others eating.
Or the homeless old women carrying
all they own in worn shopping bags
around Chicago at three in the morning.
What is the point of my suffering?
They are nothing to me. Filthy
pigeons. Jew-hating old women.
Why does it bother with me?

GAMES

Imagine if suffering were real.
Imagine if those old people were afraid of death.
What if the midget or the girl with one arm
really felt pain? Imagine how impossible it would be
to live if some people were
alone and afraid all their lives.

MY GRAVEYARD IN TOKYO

It was hard to see the moonlight
on the gravestones
because of the neon
in the parking lot.
I said I did in my letters.
But thinking back on it now,
I don't feel sure.

ALONE ON CHRISTMAS EVE IN JAPAN

Not wanting to lose it all for poetry.
Wanting to live the living. All this year
looking on the graveyard below my apartment.
Holding myself tenderly in this marred body.
Wondering if the quiet I feel is that happiness
wise people speak of, or the modulation
that is the acquiescence to death beginning.

TEXTURES

We had walked three miles through the night
when I had to piss. She stopped just beyond.
I aimed at the stone wall of a vineyard,
but the wind took it and she made a sound.
I apologized. "It's all right," she said out
of the dark, her voice different. "I liked it."

THE REVOLUTION

Robinson Crusoe breaks a plate on his way out,
and hesitates over the pieces. The ship begins
to sink as he sweeps them up. Sets the table
and stands looking at history for the last time.
Knowing precision will leak from him
however well he learns the weather or vegetation,
and despite the cunning of his hands.
His mind can survive only among the furniture.
Amid the primary colors of the island, he will
become a fine thing, perhaps, but a different one.

MEXICO

I went to sleep by the highway
and woke just before dawn,
to see people drifting toward me
across the fields. Silently
getting into trucks.
Blurred like first love.
Another inappropriate beauty
I leave out of what I am making.

ANOTHER GRANDFATHER

Every generation tells
of how the good world died.
How he went into the giant corn
at night, leaving the dogs.
Always they say it was the end
once and for all of America.
Grandfather and curing tobacco.

We picked the clumsy leaves,
sweating. And piled them on sleds.
Girls tied them in bunches
and the bunches on poles. The poles
were hung in a log barn.
He built fires underneath for days
and stayed up with the thermometer.

I was proud to be out there, but afraid
of his dogs and the size of the dark.
A city child, down for the summer.
When suddenly he walked into
the twelve-foot wall of corn.
Leaving the dogs. Firelight
on the barn. The smell of Carolina.

The stars making me lurch.
Thirty years ago. And now
loud cantons night
after night: America, America.
He came back with watermelons,
but always I see him going
into the corn. And that order ending.

SINGING IN MY DIFFICULT MOUNTAINS

Helot for what time there is
in the baptist hegemony of death.
For what time there is summer,
island, cornice. Weeping
and singing of what declines
into the earth. But of having,
not of not having. What abounds.
Amazed morning after morning
by the yielding. What times there are.
My fine house that love is.

THRESHING THE FIRE

I
Fire begins seriously at the body
and it sits up. The oldest son beats it down.
It sits up and he clubs it back again.
That's what I want.

This best time begins and stomach can't have it.
Nor pride. Nor snakebrain's excitements
and darkness. Let him hammer me down
into the paradise furnace.

The boy I was remembers the scale. Flames
two hundred feet up into the sky every night.
Three powerful rivers naked everywhere.
Brick and metal. Dirty brick and old raw iron.

He does not understand, but he knew the wanting.
Remembers working in the mill, the titanic shear
cleaving slabs into sections. Halfway
to something. Smell of Pittsburgh after rain.

Smell of winter steel and grease, and the smell
of welding. Believing there were breasts.
So he will hammer me deep into that rendering.
Knowing blindly there is something to get.

II

Love like chunks of an animal.
Clothes ripped off and clothes drawn aside.
Bodies like cries from the ocean.
Hearts like unkeeled Jerusalem.

Italian breasts under brambles in Perugia.
My youth clandestinely in the palazzo.
Stumbling into love,
bewildered by the storms of me. Soft beauty.

Beyond youth after, and my heart augmenting.
(Stronger, she said to the choir, not louder.)
Love a second time, then eight years with Linda.
Now love probably not again.

The pictures of paradise seem innocent,
and the Devil's temptation things for children.
I would burrow into stone. Into iron.
Into the rain to find someone important

there in the dark. A mystery that magnifies
the earth but does not lie. What is Pure Land
to that? Let him force me to try once more.
Insist, insist until I at least fail.

III
Cicadas on the olive trees rage in brevity.
When I go out at night, the stars and quiet
smell of jasmine and I long for a life
like fatty boiled beef. Pound me into that.

I was looking down on my Tokyo graveyard
late at night and heard in the complete
silence a violin string snap.
Drive me down there.

Lord Nobunaga (surrounded, the castle
on fire), knowing he would die that day,
put on his kimono and slowly danced the Nō
in the flames. When great Hideyoshi was shōgun

and lying on his deathbed, he wept constantly.
Saying over and over, I don't want to die.
I want to live a thousand years.
Keep me at them both.

The boy walked the mean winter streets of Pittsburgh
knowing of their leafy summer. Let him make sure
the dreams are loose before the fire gets it all.
And I am hammered into the sun.

THE GREAT FIRES:

POEMS 1982–1992

[1994]

GOING WRONG

The fish are dreadful. They are brought up
the mountain in the dawn most days, beautiful
and alien and cold from night under the sea,
the grand rooms fading from their flat eyes.
Soft machinery of the dark, the man thinks,
washing them. "What can you know of my machinery!"
demands the Lord. *Sure*, the man says quietly
and cuts into them, laying back the dozen struts,
getting to the muck of something terrible.
The Lord insists: "You are the one who chooses
to live this way. I build cities where things
are human. I make Tuscany and you go to live
with rock and silence." The man washes away
the blood and arranges the fish on a big plate.
Starts the onions in the hot olive oil and puts
in peppers. "You have lived all year without women."
He takes out everything and puts in the fish.
"No one knows where you are. People forget you.
You are vain and stubborn." The man slices
tomatoes and lemons. Takes out the fish
and scrambles eggs. *I am not stubborn*, he thinks,
laying all of it on the table in the courtyard
full of early sun, shadows of swallows flying
on the food. *Not stubborn, just greedy.*

GUILTY

The man certainly looked guilty.
Ugly, ragged, and not clean. Not to mention
their finding him there in the woods
with her body. Neighbors told how he was
always playing with dead squirrels,
mangled dogs, even snakes. He said
those were the only things that would
allow him to get close. "Look at me,"
the old man said with uncomplaining
simplicity, "I'm already one of the dead
among the dead. It's hard to watch things
humiliated the way death does it.
Possums smeared on the road, birds with ants
eating out their eyes. Even dying rats
want privacy for their disgrace.
It's true I washed the dirt from her face
and the blood off the body. Combed her hair.
I slept beside her, at her feet for two days,
the way my dog used to. I got the dress
on the best I could. She looked so neglected.
Like garbage thrown in the weeds.
Like nobody cared because he had done that
to her. I kept thinking about how long
she is going to be alone now. I knew
the police would take pictures and put them
in the papers naked and open so people
eating breakfast could look at her. I wanted
to give her spirit enough time to get ready."

How astonishing it is that language can almost mean,
and frightening that it does not quite. *Love*, we say,
God, we say, *Rome* and *Michiko*, we write, and the words
get it wrong. We say *bread* and it means according
to which nation. French has no word for home,
and we have no word for strict pleasure. A people
in northern India is dying out because their ancient
tongue has no words for endearment. I dream of lost
vocabularies that might express some of what
we no longer can. Maybe the Etruscan texts would
finally explain why the couples on their tombs
are smiling. And maybe not. When the thousands
of mysterious Sumerian tablets were translated,
they seemed to be business records. But what if they
are poems or psalms? My joy is the same as twelve
Ethiopian goats standing silent in the morning light.
O Lord, thou art slabs of salt and ingots of copper,
as grand as ripe barley lithe under the wind's labor.
Her breasts are six white oxen loaded with bolts
of long-fibered Egyptian cotton. My love is a hundred
pitchers of honey. Shiploads of thuya are what
my body wants to say to your body. Giraffes are this
desire in the dark. Perhaps the spiral Minoan script
is not a language but a map. What we feel most has
no name but amber, archers, cinnamon, horses and birds.

LOVERS

When I hear men boast about how passionate
they are, I think of the two cleaning ladies
at a second-story window watching a man
coming back from a party where there was
lots of free beer. He runs in and out
of buildings looking for a toilet. "My Lord,"
the tall woman says, "that fellow down there
surely does love architecture."

MEASURING THE TYGER

Barrels of chains. Sides of beef stacked in vans.
Water buffalo dragging logs of teak in the river mud
outside Mandalay. Pantocrator in the Byzantium dome.
The mammoth overhead crane bringing slabs of steel
through the dingy light and roar to the giant shear
that cuts the adamantine three-quarter-inch plates
and they flop down. The weight of the mind fractures
the girders and piers of the spirit, spilling out
the heart's melt. Incandescent ingots big as cars
trundling out of titanic mills, red slag scaling off
the brighter metal in the dark. The Monongahela River
below, night's sheen on its belly. Silence except
for the machinery clanging deeper in us. You will
love again, people say. Give it time. Me with time
running out. Day after day of the everyday.
What they call real life, made of eighth-inch gauge.
Newness strutting around as if it were significant.
Irony, neatness and rhyme pretending to be poetry.
I want to go back to that time after Michiko's death
when I cried every day among the trees. To the real.
To the magnitude of pain, of being that much alive.

VOICES INSIDE AND OUT

For Hayden Carruth

When I was a child, there was an old man with
a ruined horse who drove his wagon through the back
streets of our neighborhood, crying, *Iron! Iron!*
Meaning he would buy bedsprings and dead stoves.
Meaning for me, in the years since, the mind's steel
and the riveted girders of the soul. When I lived
on Île Saint-Louis, a glazier came every morning,
crying, *Vitre! Vitre!* Meaning the glass on his back,
but sounding like the swallows swooping years later
at evening outside my high windows in Perugia.
In my boyhood summers, Italian men came walking ahead
of the truck calling out the ripeness of their melons,
and old Jews slogged in the snow, crying, *Brooms! Brooms!*
Two hundred years ago, the London shop boys yelled
at people going by, *What do you lack?* A terrible
question to hear every day. "Less and less," I think.
The Brazilians say, "In this country we have everything
we need, except what we don't have."

TEAR IT DOWN

We find out the heart only by dismantling what
the heart knows. By redefining the morning,
we find a morning that comes just after darkness.
We can break through marriage into marriage.
By insisting on love we spoil it, get beyond
affection and wade mouth-deep into love.
We must unlearn the constellations to see the stars.
But going back toward childhood will not help.
The village is not better than Pittsburgh.
Only Pittsburgh is more than Pittsburgh.
Rome is better than Rome in the same way the sound
of raccoon tongues licking the inside walls
of the garbage tub is more than the stir
of them in the muck of the garbage. Love is not
enough. We die and are put into the earth forever.
We should insist while there is still time. We must
eat through the wildness of her sweet body already
in our bed to reach the body within that body.

DANTE DANCING

For Gianna Gelmetti

I

When he dances of meeting Beatrice that first time,
he is a youth, his body has no real language,
and his heart understands nothing of what has
started. Love like a summer rain after drought,
like the thin cry of a red-tailed hawk, like an angel
sinking its teeth into our throat. He has only
beginner steps to tell of the sheen inside him.
The boy Dante sees her first with the absolute love
possible only when we are ignorant of each other.
Arm across his face, he runs off. Years go by.

II

The next dance is about their meeting again. He does
an *enchaînement* around her. Beatrice's heavy hair is
dark and long. She watches with the *occhi dolci*.
His jumps are a man's jumps. His steps have become
the moves of a dancer who understands the dance.
A man who recognizes the body's greed. She is deep
in her body's heart. He is splendid. She is lost
and is led away by the aunt. Her family is careful
after that. She goes by in a carriage. He rises
on his toes, *port de bras*, his eyes desperate.
Then she is at an upstairs window of the palace.
He dances his sadness brilliantly in the moonlight
below on the empty piazza, concentrating. She moves
the curtain a little to the side, and he is happy.
It is a dream we all know, the perfection of love
that is not real. There is a fountain behind him.

III

It is a few years later and they are finally
in his simple room. His long dance of afterward
is a declaration of joy and of gratitude and devotion.
She dances strangely, putting on her clothes.
A delicate goodbye. Her soul is free now from that
kind of love. He stands motionless, bewildered,
watching her go. Then dances his grief wonderfully.

IV

We see Dante as an old man. He is a dancer who can
manage only the simple steps of the beginning.
He dances the romance lost, the love that never was,
and the great love missed because of dreaming.
First position, *entrechat*, and the smallest jumps.
The passionate quiet. The quieter and strongest.
The special sorrow of a happy, imperfect heart
that finally knows well how to dance. But does not.

THE GREAT FIRES

Love is apart from all things.
Desire and excitement are nothing beside it.
It is not the body that finds love.
What leads us there is the body.
What is not love provokes it.
What is not love quenches it.
Love lays hold of everything we know.
The passions which are called love
also change everything to a newness
at first. Passion is clearly the path
but does not bring us to love.
It opens the castle of our spirit
so that we might find the love which is
a mystery hidden there.
Love is one of many great fires.
Passion is a fire made of many woods,
each of which gives off its special odor
so we can know the many kinds
that are not love. Passion is the paper
and twigs that kindle the flames
but cannot sustain them. Desire perishes
because it tries to be love.
Love is eaten away by appetite.
Love does not last, but it is different
from the passions that do not last.
Love lasts by not lasting.
Isaiah said each man walks in his own fire
for his sins. Love allows us to walk
in the sweet music of our particular heart.

FINDING SOMETHING

I say moon is horses in the tempered dark,
because horse is the closest I can get to it.
I sit on the terrace of this worn villa the king's
telegrapher built on the mountain that looks down
on a blue sea and the small white ferry
that crosses slowly to the next island each noon.
Michiko is dying in the house behind me,
the long windows open so I can hear
the faint sound she will make when she wants
watermelon to suck or so I can take her
to a bucket in the corner of the high-ceilinged room
which is the best we can do for a chamber pot.
She will lean against my leg as she sits
so as not to fall over in her weakness.
How strange and fine to get so near to it.
The arches of her feet are like voices
of children calling in the grove of lemon trees,
where my heart is as helpless as crushed birds.

PROSPERO WITHOUT HIS MAGIC

He keeps the valley like this with his heart.
By paying attention, being capable, remembering.
Otherwise, there would be flies as big as dogs
in the vineyard, cows made entirely of maggots,
cruelty with machinery and canvas, sniggering
among the olive trees and the sea grossly vast.
He struggles to hold it right, the eight feet
of heaven by the well with geraniums and basil.
He will rejoice even if the shepherd girl
does not pass anymore at evening. And whether
or not she ate her lamb at Easter. He knows
that loneliness is our craft, that death is
God's vigorish. He does not keep it fine
by innocence or leaving things out.

FINDING EURYDICE

Orpheus is too old for it now. His famous voice is gone
and his career is past. No profit anymore from the songs
of love and grief. Nobody listens. Still, he goes on
secretly with his ruined alto. But not for Eurydice.
Not even for the pleasure of singing. He sings because
that is what he does. He sings about two elderly
Portuguese men in the hot Sacramento delta country.
How they show up every year or so, feeble and dressed
as well as their poverty allows. The husband is annoyed
each time by their coming to see his seventy-year-old
wife, who, long ago when they were putting through
the first railroads, was the most beautiful of all
the whores. Impatient, but saying nothing, he lets them
take her carefully upstairs to give her a bath. He does
not understand how much their doting eyes can see the sleek,
gleaming beauty of her hidden in the bright water.

GOING THERE

Of course it was a disaster.
That unbearable, dearest secret
has always been a disaster.
The danger when we try to leave.
Going over and over afterward
what we should have done
instead of what we did.
But for those short times
we seemed to be alive. Misled,
misused, lied to and cheated,
certainly. Still, for that
little while, we visited
our possible life.

HAUNTED IMPORTANTLY

It was in the transept of the church, winter in
the stones, the dim light brightening on her,
when Linda said, Listen. Listen to this, she said.
When he put his ear against the massive door,
there were spirits singing inside. He hunted for it
afterward. In Madrid, he heard a bell begin somewhere
in the night rain. Worked his way through
the tangle of alleys, the sound deeper and more
powerful as he got closer. Short of the plaza,
it filled all of him and he turned back. No need,
he thought, to see the bell. It was not the bell
he was trying to find, but the angel lost
in our bodies. The music that thinking is.
He wanted to know what he heard, not to get closer.

SEARCHING FOR PITTSBURGH

The fox pushes softly, blindly through me at night,
between the liver and the stomach. Comes to the heart
and hesitates. Considers and then goes around it.
Trying to escape the mildness of our violent world.
Goes deeper, searching for what remains of Pittsburgh
in me. The rusting mills sprawled gigantically
along three rivers. The authority of them.
The gritty alleys where we played every evening were
stained pink by the inferno always surging in the sky,
as though Christ and the Father were still fashioning
the Earth. Locomotives driving through the cold rain,
lordly and bestial in their strength. Massive water
flowing morning and night throughout a city
girded with ninety bridges. Sumptuous-shouldered,
sleek-thighed, obstinate and majestic, unquenchable.
All grip and flood, mighty sucking and deep-rooted grace.
A city of brick and tired wood. Ox and sovereign spirit.
Primitive Pittsburgh. Winter month after month telling
of death. The beauty forcing us as much as harshness.
Our spirits forged in that wilderness, our minds forged
by the heart. Making together a consequence of America.
The fox watched me build my Pittsburgh again and again.
In Paris afternoons on Buttes-Chaumont. On Greek islands
with their fields of stone. In beds with women, sometimes,
amid their gentleness. Now the fox will live in our ruined
house. My tomatoes grow ripe among weeds and the sound
of water. In this happy place my serious heart has made.

MARRIED

I came back from the funeral and crawled
around the apartment, crying hard,
searching for my wife's hair.
For two months got them from the drain,
from the vacuum cleaner, under the refrigerator,
and off the clothes in the closet.
But after other Japanese women came,
there was no way to be sure which were
hers, and I stopped. A year later,
repotting Michiko's avocado, I find
a long black hair tangled in the dirt.

EXPLICATING THE TWILIGHT

The rat makes her way up
the mulberry tree, the branches
getting thin and risky up close
to the fruit, and she slows.
The berry she is after is so ripe,
there is almost no red. Prospero
thinks of Christopher Smart saying
purple is black blooming. She lifts
her mouth to the berry, stretching.
The throat is an elegant gray.
A thousand shades, Christopher wrote
among the crazy people. A thousand
colors from white to silver.

STEEL GUITARS

The world is announced by the smell of oregano and sage
in rocky places high up, with white doves higher still
in the blue sky. Or the faint voices of women and girls
in the olive trees below, and a lustrous sea beneath that.
Like thoughts of lingerie while reading *Paradise Lost*
in Alabama. Or the boy in Pittsburgh that only summer
he was nine, prowling near the rusty railroad yard
where they put up vast tents and a man lifted anvils
with chains through his nipples. The boy listened
for the sound that made him shiver as he ran hard
across the new sawdust to see the two women again
on a platform above his head, indolent and almost naked
in the simple daylight. Reality stretched thin
as he watched their painted eyes brooding on what
they contained. He vaguely understood that it was not
their flesh that was a mystery but something on the other
side of it. Now the man remembering the boy knows
there is a door. We go through and hear a sound
like buildings burning, like the sound of a stone hitting
a stone in the dark. The heart in its plenty hammered
by rain and need, by the weight of what momentarily is.

RECOVERING AMID THE FARMS

Every morning the sad girl brings her three sheep
and two lambs laggardly to the top of the valley,
past my stone hut and onto the mountain to graze.
She turned twelve last year and it was legal
for the father to take her out of school. She knows
her life is over. The sadness makes her fine,
makes me happy. Her old red sweater makes
the whole valley ring, makes my solitude gleam.
I watch from hiding for her sake. Knowing I am
there is hard on her, but it is the focus of her days.
She always looks down or looks away as she passes
in the evening. Except sometimes when, just before
going out of sight behind the distant canebrake,
she looks quickly back. It is too far for me to see,
but there is a moment of white if she turns her face.

It should have been the family that lasted.
Should have been my sister and my peasant mother.
But it was not. They were the affection,
not the journey. It could have been my father,
but he died too soon. Gelmetti and Gregg
and Nogami lasted. It was the newness of me,
and the newness after that, and newness again.
It was the important love and the serious lust.
It was Pittsburgh that lasted. The iron and fog
and sooty brick houses. Not Aunt Mince and Pearl,
but the black-and-white winters with their girth
and geological length of cold. Streets ripped
apart by ice and emerging like wounded beasts when
the snow finally left in April. Freight trains
with their steam locomotives working at night.
Summers the size of crusades. When I was a boy,
I saw downtown a large camera standing in front
of the William Pitt Hotel or pointed at Kaufmann's
Department Store. Usually around midnight,
but the people still going by. The camera set
slow enough that cars and people left no trace.
The crowds in Rome and Tokyo and Manhattan
did not last. But the empty streets of Perugia,
my two bowls of bean soup on Kos, and Pimpaporn
Charionpanith lasted. The plain nakedness of Anna
in Denmark remains in me forever. The wet lilacs
on Highland Avenue when I was fourteen. Carrying
Michiko dead in my arms. It is not about the spirit.
The spirit dances, comes and goes. But the soul
is nailed to us like lentils and fatty bacon lodged

under the ribs. What lasted is what the soul ate.
The way a child knows the world by putting it
part by part into his mouth. As I tried to gnaw
my way into the Lord, working to put my heart
against that heart. Lying in the wheat at night,
letting the rain after all the dry months have me.

TO SEE IF SOMETHING COMES NEXT

There is nothing here at the top of the valley.
Sky and morning, silence and the dry smell
of heavy sunlight on the stone everywhere.
Goats occasionally, and the sound of roosters
in the bright heat where he lives with the dead
woman and purity. Trying to see if something
comes next. Wondering whether he has stalled.
Maybe, he thinks, it is like the Nō: whenever
the script says *dances*, whatever the actor does next
is a dance. If he stands still, he is dancing.

A STUBBORN ODE

All of it. The sane woman under the bed with the rat
that is licking off the peanut butter she puts on her
front teeth for him. The beggars of Calcutta blinding
their children while somewhere people are rich
and eating with famous friends and having running water
in their fine houses. Michiko is buried in Kamakura.
The tired farmers thresh barley all day under the feet
of donkeys amid the merciless power of the sun.
The beautiful women grow old, our hearts moderate.
All of us wane, knowing things could have been different.
When Gordon was released from the madhouse, he could
not find Hayden to say goodbye. As he left past
Hall Eight, he saw the face in a basement window,
tears running down the cheeks. And I say, nevertheless.

SCHEMING IN THE SNOW

There is a time after what comes after
being young, and a time after that, he thinks
happily as he walks through the winter woods,
hearing in the silence a woodpecker far off.
Remembering his Chinese friend
whose brother gave her a jade ring from
the Han Dynasty when she turned eighteen.
Two weeks later, when she was hurrying up
the steps of a Hong Kong bridge, she fell,
and the thousand-year-old ring shattered
on the concrete. When she told him, stunned
and tears running down her face, he said,
"Don't cry. I'll get you something better."

To tell the truth, Storyville was brutal. The parlors
of even the fancy whorehouses crawling with roaches
and silverfish. The streets foul and the sex brawling.
But in the shabby clapboard buildings on Franklin
and on Liberty and on Iberville was the invention.
Throughout the District, you could hear Tony Jackson
and King Oliver, Morton and Bechet finding it night
after night. Like the dream Bellocq's photographs found
in the midst of Egypt Vanita and Mary Meathouse, Aunt Cora
and Gold Tooth Gussie. It takes a long time to get
the ruins right. The Japanese think it strange we paint
our old wooden houses when it takes so long to find
the *wabi* in them. They prefer the bonsai tree after
the valiant blossoming is over, the leaves fallen. When
bareness reveals a merit born in the vegetable struggling.

BETROTHED

You hear yourself walking on the snow.
You hear the absence of the birds.
A stillness so complete, you hear
the whispering inside of you. Alone
morning after morning, and even more
at night. They say we are born alone,
to live and die alone. But they are wrong.
We get to be alone by time, by luck,
or by misadventure. When I hit the log
frozen in the woodpile to break it free,
it makes a sound of perfect inhumanity,
which goes pure all through the valley,
like a crow calling unexpectedly
at the darker end of twilight that awakens
me in the middle of a life. The black
and white of me mated with this indifferent
winter landscape. I think of the moon
coming in a little while to find the white
among these colorless pines.

TRYING TO HAVE SOMETHING LEFT OVER

There was a great tenderness to the sadness
when I would go there. She knew how much
I loved my wife and that we had no future.
We were like casualties helping each other
as we waited for the end. Now I wonder
if we understood how happy those Danish
afternoons were. Most of the time we did not talk.
Often I took care of the baby while she did
housework. Changing him and making him laugh.
I would say *Pittsburgh* softly each time before
throwing him up. Whisper *Pittsburgh* with
my mouth against the tiny ear and throw
him higher. Pittsburgh and happiness high up.
The only way to leave even the smallest trace.
So that all his life her son would feel gladness
unaccountably when anyone spoke of the ruined
city of steel in America. Each time almost
remembering something maybe important that got lost.

ON STONE

The monks petition to live the harder way,
in pits dug farther up the mountain,
but only the favored ones are permitted
that scraped life. The syrup-water and cakes
the abbot served me were far too sweet.
A simple misunderstanding of pleasure
because of inexperience. I pull water up
hand over hand from thirty feet of stone.
My kerosene lamp burns a mineral light.
The mind and its fierceness lives here in silence.
I dream of women and hunger in my valley
for what can be made of granite. Like the sun
hammering this earth into pomegranates
and grapes. Dryness giving way to the smell
of basil at night. Otherwise, the stone
feeds on stone, is reborn as rock,
and the heart wanes. Athena's owl calling
into the barrenness, and nothing answering.

RELATIVE PITCH

I was carrying supplies back up the mountain
when I heard it, the laughter of children,
so strange in that starkness.
Pushed past the brush and scrub willow
and saw a ruined farmhouse and girls
in ragged clothes. They had rigged a swing
and were playing as though they were happy,
as if they did not know any better.
Having no way to measure, I thought,
remembering the man in Virginia who found
a ruined octagonal mansion
and repaired it perfectly. For months
he walked through the grand empty rooms
wondering what they were like.
Until he found a broken chair in the attic
and re-created the colors and scale. Discovered
maybe the kind of life the house was.
Strangers leave us poems to tell of those
they loved, how the heart broke, to whisper
of the religion upstairs in the dark,
sometimes in the parlor amid blazing sunlight,
and under trees with rain coming down
in August on the bare, unaccustomed bodies.

1953

All night in the Iowa café. Friday night
and the farm boys with their pay.
Fine bodies and clean faces. All of them
proud to be drunk. No meanness,
just energy. At the next table, they talked
cars for hours, friends coming and going,
hollering over. The one with the heavy face
and pale hair kept talking about the Chevy
he had years ago and how it could
take everything in second.
Moaning that he should never have sold it.
Didn't he show old Hank? Bet your ass!
That Fourth of July when Shelvadeen
got too much patriotism and beer
and gave some to everybody
down by the river. Hank so mad because
I left him like he was standing still.
Best car that ever was, and never should have
let it go. Tears falling on his eggs.

ALONE

I never thought Michiko would come back
after she died. But if she did, I knew
it would be as a lady in a long white dress.
It is strange that she has returned
as somebody's dalmatian. I meet
the man walking her on a leash
almost every week. He says good morning
and I stoop down to calm her. He said
once that she was never like that with
other people. Sometimes she is tethered
on their lawn when I go by. If nobody
is around, I sit on the grass. When she
finally quiets, she puts her head in my lap
and we watch each other's eyes as I whisper
in her soft ears. She cares nothing about
the mystery. She likes it best when
I touch her head and tell her small
things about my days and our friends.
That makes her happy the way it always did.

ADULTERATED

Bella fica! (beautiful fig, fine sex) the whore said
in the back streets of Livorno, proudly slapping
her groin when the man tried to get the price down.
Braddock, the heavyweight champion of the world,
when Joe Louis was destroying him, blood spraying
and his manager between rounds wanting to stop
the fight, said, I won the title in the ring,
I'm going to lose it in the ring. And, after more
damage, did. Therefore does the wind keep blowing
that holds this great Earth in the air.
For this the birds sing sometimes without purpose.
We value the soiled old theaters because of what
sometimes happens there. Berlin in the thirties.
There were flowers all around Jesus in his agony
at Gethsemane. The Lord sees everything, and sees
that it is good despite everything. The manger
was filthy. The women at Dachau knew they were about
to be gassed when they pushed back the Nazi guard
who wanted to die with them, saying he must live.
And sang for a little while after the doors closed.

WHAT IS THERE TO SAY?

What do they say each new morning
in Heaven? They would
weary of one always
singing how green the
green trees are in
Paradise.

Surely it would seem convention
and affectation
to rejoice every time
Helen went by, since
she would have gone
daily by.

What can I say then each time
your whiteness glimmers
and fashions in the night?
If each time your voice
opens so near
in that dark

new? What can I say each morning
after that you will
believe? But there is this
stubborn provincial
singing in me,
O, each time.

PROSPERO DREAMS OF ARNAUT DANIEL INVENTING LOVE IN THE TWELFTH CENTURY

Let's get hold of one of those deer
that live way up there in the mountains.
Lure it down with flutes, or lasso
it from helicopters, or just take it out
with a .30-30. Anyhow, we get one.
Then we reach up inside its ass and maybe
find us a little gland or something
that might make a hell of a perfume.
It's worth a try. You never know.

Not the river as fact, but the winter river,
and that river in June as two rivers.
We feel it run through our nature, the water
smelling of wet rotting just before spring,
and we call it love, a wilderness in the mind.
Mediterranean light as provender of women.
All of it contingent. This version of me
differs from another version as a vector product.
The body is a condition of the spirit.
The snow sifts down from the pines in the noon
and makes the silence even louder. A tumult
of singing when we cross the border of courtesy
into a savor of the heart. Each of us tempered
by the other, altered in ways more truly us.
We go into the secret with the shades pulled
down at dawn. Like a house on fire in sunlight.
We enable God to finally understand there is
a difference between you sitting in the clearing
confused by moonlight and you sitting in the bare
farmhouse amid the kerosene light. The two of you.

CARRYING TORCHES AT NOON

The boy came home from school and found a hundred lamps
filling the house. Lamps everywhere and all turned on
despite the summer shining in the handsome windows.
Two and three lamps on every table. Lamps in chairs
and on the rugs and even in the kitchen. More lamps
upstairs and on the topmost floor as well. All brightly
burning, until the police came and took them away.
An excess of light that continued in him for a long time.
That radiance of lamps flourishing in the day became
a benchmark for his heart, became a Beaufort scale
for his appetites. The wildness and gladness of it,
the illicitness in him magnified the careful gleam
of Paris mornings when he got to them, and the dark
glisten of the Seine each night as he crossed
the stone bridges back to his room. It was the same
years later as the snow fell through the bruised light
of a winter afternoon and he stood in a narrow street
telling Anna he was leaving. All of it a light beyond
anybody's ability to manage. The Massachusetts sunlight
lies comfortably on the maples. The Pittsburgh lamps
inside of him make it look maybe not good enough.

A YEAR LATER

For Linda Gregg

From this distance they are unimportant
standing by the sea. She is weeping, wearing
a white dress, and the marriage is almost over,
after eight years. All around is the flat
uninhabited side of the island. The water
is blue in the morning air. They did not know
this would happen when they came, just the two
of them and the silence. A purity that looked
like beauty and was too difficult for people.

LOOKING AWAY FROM LONGING

On Fish Mountain, she has turned away
from the temple where they painted
pictures of Paradise everywhere inside
so that a population who prayed only
not to live could imagine yearning.
She is looking at a tree instead.
Below is a place where the man
and the beautiful woman will eat
cold noodles almost outside on a hot day.
Below that is the sound of fast water
with a barefoot woman beside it beating
an octopus on the wet stones. And then
the floor of the valley opening out onto
the yellow of blooming mustard and smoke
going straight up from large farmhouses
in the silent early evening. Where they
will walk through all of it slowly,
not talking much. A small him
and a smaller her with long black hair,
so happy together, beginning the trip
toward where she will die and leave him
looking at the back of her turned away
looking at a small tree.

FACTORING

"Barefoot farm girls in silk dresses," he thinks.
Meaning Marie Antoinette and the nobles
at Versailles playing at the real world.
Thinking about the elaborate seduction of ladies
and their languorous indifference in complying.
"Labored excess," he mutters, remembering
the modern Japanese calligraphers straining
at deliberate carelessness. He is still
waiting for his strange heart to moderate.
"Love as two spirits merging," he thinks,
"the flesh growing luminous and then transparent.
Who could deal with that? Like a summer lake
flickering through pine trees." It says
in Ecclesiastes that everything has its season.
A time to scatter stones and a time to gather them.
He used to wonder about the proper occasion
for casting away stones, whether it might
mean desire. He wonders if Pimpaporn went back
to her village, pictures the jungle and houses
made of teak on stilts. Tries to understand that
as a real world. Tries to know her belatedly.
He thinks of the multitude of giant rats he killed
in those cavernous, Sunday-empty, neon-dark
steel mills. Remembers piling them up
on winter nights, the weight of each, one after
the other. White mist on the black river outside.

THE MILK OF PARADISE

On the beach below Sperlonga everyone else is
speaking Italian, lazily paradisal in the heat.
He tries to make something of it, as though
something were going on. As though there were
something to be found in the obvious nakedness
of breasts. He complicates what is easily true,
hunting it down. It matters disproportionately
to him to see the ocean suddenly as he turns over.
He watches the afternoon as though it had
a secret. For years he will be considering
the two women nearby who decide to get lunch
at the restaurant back by the cliff. The taller
one picks up her top and tries to get
into it as they start out. But it tangles,
and she gives it indolently to the prettier one,
who puts it on as they walk away carelessly
into the garnishing Mediterranean light.

GIFT HORSES

He lives in the barrens, in dying neighborhoods
and negligible countries. None with an address.
But still the Devil finds him. Kills the wife
or spoils the marriage. Publishes each place
and makes it popular, makes it better, makes it
unusable. Brings news of friends, all defeated,
most sick or sad without reasons. Shows him
photographs of the beautiful women in old movies
whose luminous faces sixteen feet tall looked out
at the boy in the dark where he grew his heart.
Brings pictures of what they look like now.
Says how lively they are, and brave despite their age.
Taking away everything. For the Devil is commissioned
to harm, to keelhaul us with loss, with knowledge
of how all things splendid are disfigured by small
and small. Yet he allows us to eat roast goat
on the mountain above Parakia. Lets us stumble
for the first time, unprepared, onto the buildings
of Palladio in moonlight. Maybe because he is not
good at his job. I believe he loves us against
his will. Because of the women and how the men
struggle to hear inside them. Because we construe
something important from trees and locomotives,
smell weeds on a hot July afternoon and are augmented.

HARD WIRED

He is shamelessly happy to feel the thing
inside him. He labors up through the pines
with firewood and goes back down again.
Winter on the way. Roses and blackberries
finished, and the iris gone before that.
The peas dead in the garden and the beans
almost done. His tomatoes are finally ripe.
The thing is inside him like that, and will
come back. An old thing, a dangerous one.
Precious to him. He meets the raccoon often
in the dark and ends up throwing stones.
The raccoon gets behind a tree. Comes again,
cautious and fierce. It stops halfway.
They stand glaring in the faint starlight.

The snow falling around the man in the naked woods
is like the ash of heaven, ash from the cool fire
of God's mother-of-pearl, moon-stately heart.
Sympathetic but not merciful. His strictness
parses us. The discomfort of living this way
without birds, among maples without leaves, makes
death and the world visible. Not the harshness,
but the way this world can be known by pushing
against it. And feeling something pushing back.
The whiteness of the winter married to this river
makes the water look black. The water actually
is the color of giant mirrors set along the marble
corridors of the spirit, the mirrors empty
of everything. The man is doing the year's accounts.
Finding the balance, trying to estimate how much
he has been translated. For it does translate him,
well or poorly. As the woods are translated
by the seasons. He is searching for a baseline
of the Lord. He searches like the blind man
going forward with a hand stretched out in front.
As the truck driver ice-fishing on the big pond
tries to learn from his line what is down there.
The man attends to any signal that might announce
Jesus. He hopes for even the faintest evidence,
the presence of the Lord's least abundance. He measures
with tenderness, afraid to find a heart more classical
than ripe. Hoping for honey, for love's alembic.

MICHIKO NOGAMI (1946–1982)

Is she more apparent because she is not
anymore forever? Is her whiteness more white
because she was the color of pale honey?
A smokestack making the sky more visible.
A dead woman filling the whole world. Michiko
said, "The roses you gave me kept me awake
with the sound of their petals falling."

THE CONTAINER FOR THE THING CONTAINED

What is the man searching for inside her blouse?
He has been with her body for seven years
and still is surprised by the arches of her
slender feet. He still traces her spine
with careful attention, feeling for the bones
of her pelvic girdle when he arrives there.
Her flesh is bright in sunlight and then not
as he leans forward and back. Picasso in his later
prints shows himself as a grotesque painter
watching closely a young Spanish woman on the bed
with her legs open and the old duenna in black
to the side. He had known nakedness every day
for sixty years. What could there be in it still
to find? But he was happy even then to get
close to the distant, distant intermittency.
Like a piano playing faintly on a second floor
in a back room. The music seems familiar, but is not.

Mogins disliked everything about Anna's pregnancy.
Said it was organs and fluids and stuff no man wanted
to know about. He was so disturbed by her milkiness
after the birth that he took his class to another part
of Denmark for the summer. When we finally made love,
the baby began to cry, and I went to get him. Anna held
the boy as we continued, until the strength went out
of her and I cradled his nakedness asleep against me
as we passed through the final stages. In the happiness
afterward, both of us nursed at her, our heads
nudging each other blindly in the brilliant dark.

THE LORD SITS WITH ME OUT IN FRONT

The Lord sits with me out in front watching
a sweet darkness begin in the fields.
We try to decide whether I am lonely.
I tell about waking at four a.m. and thinking
of what the man did to the daughter of Louise.
And there being no moon when I went outside.
He says maybe I am getting old.
That being poor is taking too much out of me.
I say I am fine. He asks for the Brahms.
We watch the sea fade. The tape finishes again
and we sit on. Unable to find words.

BETWEEN AGING AND OLD

I wake up like a stray dog
belonging to no one.
Cold, cold, and the rain.
Friendships outgrown or ruined.
And love, dear God, the women
I have loved now only names
remembered: dead, lost, or old.
Mildness more and more the danger.
Living among rocks and weeds
to guard against wisdom.
Alone with the heart howling
and refusing to let it feed on
mere affection. Lying in the dark,
singing about the intractable
kinds of happiness.

It thrashes in the oaks and soughs in the elms,
catches on innocence and soon dismantles that.
Sends children bewildered into life. Childhood
ends and is not buried. The young men ride out
and fall off, the horses wandering away. They get
on boats, are carried downstream, discover maidens.
They marry them without meaning to, meaning no harm,
the language beyond them. So everything ends.
Divorce gets them nowhere. They drift away from
the ruined women without noticing. See birds
high up and follow. "Out of earshot," they think,
puzzled by *earshot*. History driving them forward,
making a noise like the wind in maples, of women
in their dresses. It stings their hearts finally.
It wakes them up, baffled in the middle of their lives
on a small bare island, the sea blue and empty,
the days stretching all the way to the horizon.

OLDER WOMEN

Each farmer on the island conceals
his hive far up on the mountain,
knowing it will otherwise be plundered.
When they die, or can no longer make
the hard climb, the lost combs year
after year grow heavier with honey.
And the sweetness has more and more
acutely the taste of that wilderness.

EXCEEDING

Flying up, crossing over, going forward.
Passing through, getting deep enough. Breaking
into, finding the way, living at the heart
and going beyond that. Finally realizing
that arriving is not the same as being resident.
That what we do is not what we are doing.
We go into the orchard for apples. But what
we carry back is the day among trees with odor,
coolness, dappled light and time. The season
and geese going over. Always and always
with death to come, and before that the dishonor
of growing old. But meanwhile the trees are
heavy with ripe fruit. We try to visit Greece
and find ourselves instead in the pointless noon
standing among vetch and grapes, disassembling
as night climbs beautifully out of the earth
and God holds His breath. In the distance there is
the faint clatter of a farmer's bucket as she
gets water up at the well for the animals.

INFIDELITY

He stands freezing in the dark courtyard looking up
at their bright windows, as he has many nights since
moving away. Because of his promise, he does not
go up. He is thinking of the day she came back
from the hospital. They did not know her then.
He was looking down because of the happiness in her
voice talking to her husband as they went across
the courtyard. She saw him and, grinning, held up
the newborn child. Now it is the last time ever.
He finally knocks. Her eyes widen when she opens
the door. She looks to indicate her husband is home
as she unbuttons her dress. He whispers that his hands
are too cold. It will make me remember better,
she says, and puts them on her nakedness, wincing,
eyes wild with love. It is snowing when he leaves,
the narrow street lit here and there by shop windows.
Tomorrow he will be on the train with his wife, watching
the shadows on the snow. Going south to live silently
with perfect summer skies and the brilliant Aegean.

We think of lifetimes as mostly the exceptional
and sorrows. Marriage we remember as the children,
vacations, and emergencies. The uncommon parts.
But the best is often when nothing is happening.
The way a mother picks up the child almost without
noticing and carries her across Waller Street
while talking with the other woman. What if she
could keep all of that? Our lives happen between
the memorable. I have lost two thousand habitual
breakfasts with Michiko. What I miss most about
her is that commonplace I can no longer remember.

PEACHES

The ship goes down and everybody is lost, or is living
comfortably in Spain. He finds himself at the edge
of emptiness, absence and heat everywhere.
Just shacks along the beach and nobody in them.
He has listened to the song so often that he hears
only the spaces between the notes. He stands there,
remembering peaches. A strange, almost gray kind
that had little taste when he got them home, and that
little not much good. But there had to be a reason
why people bought them. So he decided to make jam.
When he smelled the scorching, they were already tar.
Scraped out the mess and was glad to have it over.
Found himself licking the crust on the spoon. Next day
he had eaten the rest, still not sure whether he liked
it or not. And never able to find any of them since.

MUSIC IS THE MEMORY OF WHAT
NEVER HAPPENED

We stopped to eat cheese and tomatoes and bread
so good it made me foolish. The woman with me
wanted to go through the palace of the papal
captivity. Hazley and Stern said they were going
to the whorehouse. That surprised me twice
because it was only two in the afternoon.
The woman and I went to the empty palace
and met them later to drive on. They said
how neat and clean it was in the whorehouse,
and how all the men and most of the women had
been in the fourth grade together. I remember
the soft way they said it but not what they told
about going upstairs. It is not the going instead
to a blank palace where history had left no smell
that I regret. It is not even the dream
of a Mediterranean woman pulling off her dress,
the long tousled dark hair, or even the white
teeth in the shuttered room as she smiled
mischievously at the young American. I regret
the fresh coolness when they went inside from
the July heat and everybody talking quietly
as they drank ordinary wine in that promised land.

ALTERNATIVES

It was half a palace, half an ancient fort,
and built of mud. The home of a fierce baroness.
The rest were men, mostly elderly, and all German.
When Denise arrived, it woke them from their habits.
Not because she was exciting, since the men were
only interested in boys. But soon they were taking
turns choosing her costumes and displaying her
on low couches, or half asleep in nests of cushions
on the wonderful rugs. They did not want her naked
unless covered with jewelry. Always coaxed
her to sing, to have the awkwardness and the way
she sang off-key mix with the nipples so evident,
the heavy skirts rucked up. It dominated
the evenings. They insisted she tell stories
but did not listen to the rambling accounts
of growing up in Zurich. Two were interested
in the year she modeled for *Vogue*. More responded
to the life in Paris: fancy dinners where
perfectly dressed men and women made love to her
with hands and mouths and delicate silver instruments.
For the Germans, decadence was undistinguished,
but it mattered when they recognized the names
of nobles, the painters, and the young *couturière*
who was the sensation of that season.
What Denise remembers most from the nights
is how they ended. She and the man with her
would each choose a lad and go up to the bedroom
with the wild lamentation of the unchosen following
behind them. Most had never seen a beautiful woman.
None had seen a white one. They were desperate
in their loss. When the boys were forced out,
they pounded on the great door, a thunder searching
through the empty corridors. Some went around

to the side where her window was. Swarmed up
each other's back until there were lines up the wall
six and seven bodies high. When one reached the sill
he fell immediately, because the seeing was so intense.
A long wail and a thud, and then the whimpering
and barking began again. But what she dreams of
is the first time the Germans took her to the river.
Small figures appeared in the distance. Drifted
silently across the desert, slowly through the blur
of the heat. Soon she could see how young they were.
A few riding on horses. All discarding their clothes
as they got closer to the water. Wading, swimming
across. The black horses splashing. Stopping
in a ragged line, waiting to be chosen
for the later choosing. Mostly now she dreams
of those motionless figures in the powerful emptiness.
Wordless, shining, staring at her out of their blank faces.

MICHIKO DEAD

He manages like somebody carrying a box
that is too heavy, first with his arms
underneath. When their strength gives out,
he moves the hands forward, hooking them
on the corners, pulling the weight against
his chest. He moves his thumbs slightly
when the fingers begin to tire, and it makes
different muscles take over. Afterward,
he carries it on his shoulder, until the blood
drains out of the arm that is stretched up
to steady the box and the arm goes numb. But now
the man can hold underneath again, so that
he can go on without ever putting the box down.

GHOSTS

I heard a noise this morning and found two old men
leaning on the wall of my vineyard, looking out
over the fields, silent. Went back to my desk
until somebody raised the trap door of the well.
It was the one with the cane, looking down inside.
But I was annoyed when the locked door rattled where
the grain and wine were. Went to the kitchen window
and stared at him. He said something in Greek.
I spread my arms to ask what he was doing.
He explained about growing up out there long ago.
That now they were making a little walk among
the old places. Telling it with his hands.
He made a final gesture, rubbing the side
of the first finger against that of the other hand.
I think it meant how much he felt about being here
again. We smiled, even though he was half blind.
Later, my bucket banged and I saw the heavy one
pulling up water. He cleaned the mule's stone basin
carefully with his other hand. Put back a rock
for the doves to stand on and poured in fresh water.
Stayed there, touching the old letters cut in the marble.
I watched them go slowly down the lane and out
of sight. They did not look back. As I typed,
I listened for the dog at each farm to tell me
which house they went to next. But the dogs did not
bark all the way down the long bright valley.

HARM AND BOON IN THE MEETINGS

We think the fire eats the wood.
We are wrong. The wood reaches out
to the flame. The fire licks at
what the wood harbors, and the wood
gives itself away to that intimacy,
the manner in which we and the world
meet each new day. Harm and boon
in the meetings. As heart meets what
is not heart, the way the spirit
encounters the flesh and the mouth meets
the foreignness in another mouth. We stand
looking at the ruin of our garden
in the early dark of November, hearing crows
go over while the first snow shines coldly
everywhere. Grief makes the heart
apparent as much as sudden happiness can.

MAN AT A WINDOW

He stands there baffled by pleasure and how little
it counts. The long woman is finally asleep on the bed,
the sweat beautiful on her New England nakedness.
It was while he was walking toward the shuttered window
with sunlight blazing behind it that something
important happened. He looks down through the gap
between the shutters at the Romans and late summer
in the via del Corso, trying to find a name for it,
knowing it is not love. Nor tenderness. He considers
other times just after, the random intensity sliding away,
unrecoverable. It is the sorrow that stays clear.
This specialness inside his spirit is bonded to
a knowing he cannot remember. When he was crushed,
each minor shift of his body traced out the bones
with agony, making his skeleton more and more clear
inside him. As though floodlit. He remembers
the intricate way he would lift his arm from the bed
in the hospital, turning his hand cautiously this way
and that to find the bearable paths through the air,
discovering an inch here and there where the pain
was missing. Or the cold and hunger as he walked
the alleys all night that winter down by the docks
of Genoa until each dawn, when he held the hot bowls
of tripe in his numb hands, the steam rising into his face
as he drank, the tears mixing with happiness. He opens
the shutters, and the shutters of the other window,
so the Mediterranean light can get to her. Desperately
trying to break the code while there is still time.

SONATINA

She told about when the American soldiers
came to the island. How the spirits would cling
to the wire fence and watch their bigness
and blondness, often without shirts, working
in the sunlight. So different from reality.
So innocent and laughing, as though it were
simple to be happy and kind. And their smell!
They had a smell that made the spirits shiver
and yearn to be material. She said that
the spirits would push long thin poles,
ivory in the moonlight, silently through
the fence, trying to touch the whiteness
those sleeping men had around their hearts.

FORAGING FOR WOOD ON THE MOUNTAIN

The wild up here is not creatures, wooded,
tangled wild. It is absence wild.
Barren, empty, stone wild. Worn-away wild.
Only the smell of weeds and hot air.
But a place where differences are clear.
Between the mind's severity and its harshness.
Between honesty and the failure of belief.
A man said no person is educated who knows
only one language, for he cannot distinguish
between his thought and the English version.
Up here he is translated to a place where it is
possible to discriminate between age and sorrow.

IN UMBRIA

Once upon a time I was sitting outside the café
watching twilight in Umbria when a girl came
out of the bakery with the bread her mother wanted.
She did not know what to do. Already bewildered
by being thirteen and just that summer a woman,
she now had to walk past the American.
But she did fine. Went by and around the corner
with style, not noticing me. Almost perfect.
At the last instant could not resist darting a look
down at her new breasts. Often I go back
to that dip of her head when people talk
about this one or that one of the great beauties.

CONCEIVING HIMSELF

Night after night after hot night in the clearing.
Stars, odor of damp grass, the faint sound of waves.
The palm trees around hardly visible, and the smell
of the jungle beyond. Hour after hour of the drumming
on bells, while young girls danced elegantly in their
heavy golden costumes. Afterward, groping his way
back along the dirt paths through blackness, dazed
by the trembling music, the dancing, and their hands.
(Pittsburgh so long ago. The spoor of someone inside
him. Knowing it sometimes waiting for a train in snow,
or just a moment while eating figs in a stony field.)
One evening the rain spilled down and he ran into
the tent behind the altar, where dancers and musicians
crowded together in the unnatural light of a Coleman
lantern: the girls undressing, rain in their hair,
the delicate faces still painted, their teeth white
as they laughed. None speaking English, their language
impossible. The man finally backstage in his life.

CHASTITY

A boy sits on the porch of a wooden house,
reading *War and Peace*.
Down below, it is Sunday afternoon in August.
The street is deserted except
for the powerful sun. There is a sound,
and he looks. At the bottom of the long
flight of steps, a man has fallen.
The boy gets up, not wanting to.
All year he has thought about honesty,
and he sits down. Two people finally come
and call the ambulance.
But too late. When everybody is gone,
he reads some pages, and stops.
Sits a moment, turns back to the place,
and starts again.

ME AND CAPABLANCA

The sultry first night of July, he on the bed
reading one of Chandler's lesser novels.
What he should be doing is in the other room.
Today he began carrying wood up from the valley,
already starting on winter. He closes the book
and goes naked into the pitch pines and the last
half-hour of the dark. Rain makes a sound
on the birches and a butternut tree. There is not
enough time left to use it for dissatisfaction.
Often it is hard to know when the middle game
is over and the end game beginning, the pure part
that is made more of craft than it is of magic.

A GHOST SINGS, A DOOR OPENS

Maybe when something stops, something lost in us
can be heard, like the young woman's voice that
seemed to come from an upstairs screened porch.
There were no lights in the house, nor in the other
houses, at almost one o'clock. The muffled sweet
moans changed as she changed from what she was not
into the more she was. The small panting became
the gasping. Never getting loud but growing
ever more evident in the leafy summer street.
Whimpers and keening, a perishing, then nothing.
In the silence, the man outside began to unravel,
maybe altering. Maybe altering more than that.

I IMAGINE THE GODS

I imagine the gods saying, We will
make it up to you. We will give you
three wishes, they say. Let me see
the squirrels again, I tell them.
Let me eat some of the great hog
stuffed and roasted on its giant spit
and put out, steaming, into the winter
of my neighborhood when I was usually
too broke to afford even the hundred grams
I ate so happily walking up the cobbles,
past the Street of the Moon
and the Street of the Birdcage-Makers,
the Street of Silence and the Street
of the Little Pissing. We can give you
wisdom, they say in their rich voices.
Let me go at last to Hugette, I say,
the Algerian student with her huge eyes
who timidly invited me to her room
when I was too young and bewildered
that first year in Paris.
Let me at least fail at my life.
Think, they say patiently, we could
make you famous again. Let me fall
in love one last time, I beg them.
Teach me mortality, frighten me
into the present. Help me to find
the heft of these days. That the nights
will be full enough and my heart feral.

THINKING ABOUT ECSTASY

Gradually he could hear her. Stop, she was saying,
stop! And found the bed full of glass,
his ankles bleeding, driven through the window
of her cupola. California summer. That was pleasure.
He knows about that: stained glass of the body
lit by our lovely chemistry and neural ghost.
Pleasure as fruit and pleasure as ambush. Excitement
a wind so powerful, we cannot find a shape for it,
so our apparatus cannot hold on to the brilliant
pleasure for long. Enjoyment is different.
It understands and keeps. The having of the having.
But ecstasy is a question. Doubling sensation
is merely arithmetic. If ecstasy means we are
taken over by something, we become an occupied
country, the audience to an intensity we are
only the proscenium for. The man does not want
to know rapture by standing outside himself.
He wants to know delight as the native land he is.

Light is too bare, too simple for her. She has lived
in the darkness so long, she prefers it. Sits among
the shrubs in the woods at night, singing of Orpheus,
who sings prettily but innocently. She knows we are
rendered by time, by pain and desire, so makes a home
always in the present. He still dotes on what was lost
and the losing of it, his cracked voice singing of his
young voice singing about love. The dark has derived
an excitement from her. Eurydice sings of passion
as a foreign country. Says candles made from birds
and tigers, from tallow of fox and snake, burn with
a troubling radiance. Orpheus sings about the smell
of basil growing in the rusting five-gallon can
on the wall between his vineyard and the well.
Eurydice tells of animals searching each other
on the bed meanwhile, shameful and vibrant.
He sings of soup cooking in the dented pot.
Of how fine it was out there in the stony fields,
eating and grieving and solitary year after year.

EATING WITH THE EMPEROR

Sixteen years old, surrounded by beasts in the pens
at two in the morning. The animals invisible.
Clumsy sounds of their restlessness in the dark.
Touching them. Not for the risk, but for the clues.
Not for the danger. Searching into the difference,
and the smell of wildness all around. The stink
of yaks and hyenas, the wet breathing of buffalo.
There is no handbook, no map for his heart in there,
no atlas for his spirit ever. The only geography
we have is the storybooks of our childhood. We go
step by step, mouthful and handful at a time.
Is this an apple? Yes, it tastes like an apple.
The Bible says the good place is somewhere else.
This somewhere else is certainly not that one.
He had no hope of getting to what he seemed to be.
When I think of him among camels, tapirs, and llamas,
it reminds me of the banquets of Japanese emperors.
Each dish of marvelous food was put in front of
the guest and, after a while, taken away untouched.
Course after course. I remember that youth I was
and wonder if it is the same way with the soul.
They never learned whether the emperor's food was
just much better or if it was something beyond that.
We end up asking what our lives really tasted like.

PLAYING HOUSE

I found another baby scorpion today. Tiny,
exquisite, and this time without his mother.
Alone in a bag of onions. I wonder
what was between them, this mother and babe.
Does she grieve now someplace up there hanging
by her claws as she makes her way awkwardly
back and forth across my bamboo ceiling?
Is there a bewildered sound? Like the goat
calling her eaten kid for three long days.
Is there a thin, whispery voice I can't hear
going back and forth? Which the Chinese Elm
hears. Which the grapes and ants, the spiders
and the rat I won't let in hear. Or is it insectal?
The sound of apparatus? Did she feed him incidentally
beside her? Did they sleep unafraid? Merely alert?
Not needing to touch the other first?

How could he later on believe it was the best
time when his wife died unexpectedly
and he wandered every day among the trees, crying
for more than a year? He is still alone and poor
on the island with wildflowers waist-deep
around his stone hut. In June the wind will
praise the barley stretching all the way
to the mountain. Then it will be good
in the harvested fields, with the sun nailed
to the stony earth. Mornings will come and go
in the silence, the moon a heaven mediated
by owls in the dark. Is there a happiness
later on that is neither fierce nor reasonable?
A time when the heart is fresh again, and a time
after that when the heart is ripe? The Aegean
was blue just then at the end of the valley,
and is blue now differently.

THEORETICAL LIVES

All that remains from the work of Skopas
are the feet. Sometimes not even that.
Sometimes only irregularities on the plinth
that may indicate how the figure stood.
Using the feet, or shadows of feet,
and the exact diagrams of German professors,
learned men argue about what the arms
were doing and how good the sculpture was.
As we do with our lives, guessing whether
the woman was truly happy when it rained
and if her father was really the ambassador.
Whether she was passionate or just wanted to please.

FROM THESE NETTLES, ALMS

They dragged me down. Down the muddy hill
with me frantically digging in my heels,
grabbing at bushes and weeds. Kicking
and bellowing, I was pulled down and under
the bridge. Dead for sure, I thought,
now that I was out of sight. They had me on
my back and were stomping, driving in
their heavy shoes and hurting me
with their fists. Me yelling no! no! no!
and twisting away, furious. And them,
furious, trying to kill me now because
I was too dumb to give in. Afterward,
sitting at the bus stop cleaning off
the blood, something in me wanted to know
what I was like in the middle of it,
down there under the bridge.

HOT NIGHTS IN FLORIDA

The woman is asleep in the bedroom. The fan is making
its sound and the television is on behind him
with the sound off. The chuck-will's-widow is calling
in the scrub across the asphalt road. Farther on,
the people are asleep in their one-story houses
with the lawn outside and the boat in the driveway.
He is thinking of the British Museum. These children
drive fast when they are awake. Twenty years ago
this was a swamp with alligators and no shape.
He is thinking of the Danish cold that forced him
into the gypsy girl's bed. Like walking through
a door and finding Venezia when he thought he was
in Yugoslavia. The people here seem hardly here
at all: blond desire always in the middle of
air conditioning. He remembers love as it could be.
Outside, the moon is shining on nothing in particular.

GETTING IT ALL

The air this morning is pleasant and praises nothing.
It lies easily on each thing. The light has no agency.
In this kind of world, we are on our own: the plain
black shoes of a man sitting in the doorway,
pleats of the tall woman's blue skirt as she hurries
to an office farther on. We will notice maybe
the gold-leaf edges of a book carried by the student
glinting intermittently as she crosses into the bright
sunlight on our side of the street. But usually
we depend on meditation and having things augmented.
We see the trees in their early-spring greenness,
but not again until just before winter. The common
is mostly beyond us. Love after the fervor, the wife
after three thousand nights. It is easy to realize
the horses suddenly running through an empty alley.
But marriage is clear. Like the faint sound of a cello
very late at night somewhere below in the stillness
of an old building on a street named Gernesgade.

I light the lamp and look at my watch.
Four-thirty. Tap out my shoes
because of the scorpions, and go out
into the field. Such a sweet night.
No moon, but urgent stars. Go back inside
and make hot chocolate on my butane burner.
I search around with the radio through
the skirl of the Levant. "Tea for Two"
in German. Finally, Cleveland playing
the Rams in the rain. It makes me feel
acutely here and everybody somewhere else.

LEPORELLO ON DON GIOVANNI

Do you think it's easy for him, the poor bastard?
To be that weak whenever their music begins?
It's not a convenient delight, not a tempered scale.
Not a choice. As Saint Francis had no choice,
needing to be walled up in his stone cell all winter.
To be flogged through Assisi naked and foul.
God is not optional when faith is like that.
But Francis had a vocation, not a need for silly women.
Giovanni really believes they are important.
Talks about them as parallel systems. Crazy stuff.
An educated gentleman of the finest family
wandering off helplessly after their faintest glimmer.
He believes there is a secret melded with the ladies.
He smiles and nods all evening as he listens
to their chatter and the whining about their husbands.
He says the world changes because of them.
Their flesh unfolds and he goes through to something
beyond the flesh. Hears a voice, he says.
A primitive radio at the core of them.
Growing and fading, as though it comes from the moon.

FIRST TIMES

I had not seen her for twenty years when she called
to welcome me back to America, wanting to see me.
Warning that she was past forty now and the mother
of a seven-year-old. The lost time flooded me.
Paris and me without money or a place to take her.
I borrowed a room and lit candles and had wine.
It went badly. My knees kept sliding away under me
on the starched sheets. I managed the humiliation
by turning my back and refusing to talk. She was
as young as I was and felt, I suspect, relief.

HALF THE TRUTH

The birds do not sing in these mornings. The skies
are white all day. The Canadian geese fly over
high up in the moonlight with the lonely sound
of their discontent. Going south. Now the rains
and soon the snow. The black trees are leafless,
the flowers gone. Only cabbages are left
in the bedraggled garden. Truth becomes visible,
the architecture of the soul begins to show through.
God has put off his panoply and is at home with us.
We are returned to what lay beneath the beauty.
We have resumed our lives. There is no hurry now.
We make love without rushing and find ourselves
afterward with someone we know well. Time to be
what we are getting ready to be next. This loving,
this relishing, our gladness, this being puts down
roots and comes back again year after year.

RESPECT

For Albert Schweitzer

This morning I found a baby scorpion,
perfect, in the saucepan.
Killed it with a piece of marble.

THE LIVES OF FAMOUS MEN

Trying to scrape the burned soup from my only pan
with a spoon after midnight by oil lamp
because if I do not cook the mackerel
this hot night it will kill me tomorrow
in the vegetable stew. Which is twice
wasteful. Though it would be another way
of cutting down, I am thinking, as I go out to get
more water from the well and happen to look up
through the bright stars. Yes, yes, I say,
and go on pulling at the long rope.

GETTING OLD

The soft wind comes sweet in the night
on the mountain. Invisible except for
the sound it makes in the big poplars outside
and the feel on his naked, single body,
which breathes quietly a little before dawn,
eyes open and in love with the table
and chair in the transparent dark and stars
in the other window. Soon it will be time
for the first tea and cool pear and then
the miles down and miles up the mountain.
"Old and alone," he thinks, smiling.
Full of what abundance has done to his spirit.
Feeling around inside to see if his heart
is still, thank God, ambitious. The way
old men look in their eyes each morning.
Knowing she isn't there and how much Michiko
isn't anywhere. The eyes close as he remembers
seeing the big owl on the roof last night
for the first time after hearing it for months.
Thinking how much he has grown unsuited
for love the size it is for him. "But maybe
not," he says. And the eyes open as he
grins at the heart's stubborn pretending.

HOW TO LOVE THE DEAD

She lives, the bird says, and means nothing
silly. She is dead and available,
the fox says, knowing about the spirits.
Not the picture at the funeral,
not the object of grieving. She is dead
and you can have that, he says. If you can
love without politeness or delicacy,
the fox says, love her with your wolf heart.
As the dead are to be desired.
Not the way long marriages are,
nothing happening again and again.
Not in the woods or in the fields.
Not in the cities. The painful love of being
permanently unhoused. Not color, but the stain.

ALMOST HAPPY

The goldfish is dead this morning on the bottom
of her world. The autumn sky is white,
the trees are coming apart in the cold rain.
Loneliness gets closer and closer.
He drinks hot tea and sings off-key:
This train ain't a going-home train, this train.
This is not a going-home train, this train.
This train ain't a going-home train 'cause
my home's on a gone-away train. That train.

REFUSING

HEAVEN

{2005}

A BRIEF FOR THE DEFENSE

Sorrow everywhere. Slaughter everywhere. If babies
are not starving someplace, they are starving
somewhere else. With flies in their nostrils.
But we enjoy our lives because that's what God wants.
Otherwise the mornings before summer dawn would not
be made so fine. The Bengal tiger would not
be fashioned so miraculously well. The poor women
at the fountain are laughing together between
the suffering they have known and the awfulness
in their future, smiling and laughing while somebody
in the village is very sick. There is laughter
every day in the terrible streets of Calcutta,
and the women laugh in the cages of Bombay.
If we deny our happiness, resist our satisfaction,
we lessen the importance of their deprivation.
We must risk delight. We can do without pleasure,
but not delight. Not enjoyment. We must have
the stubbornness to accept our gladness in the ruthless
furnace of this world. To make injustice the only
measure of our attention is to praise the Devil.
If the locomotive of the Lord runs us down,
we should give thanks that the end had magnitude.
We must admit there will be music despite everything.
We stand at the prow again of a small ship
anchored late at night in the tiny port
looking over to the sleeping island: the waterfront
is three shuttered cafés and one naked light burning.
To hear the faint sound of oars in the silence as a rowboat
comes slowly out and then goes back is truly worth
all the years of sorrow that are to come.

"And," she said, "you must talk no more
about ecstasy. It is a loneliness."
The woman wandered about picking up
her shoes and silks. "You said you loved me,"
the man said. "We tell lies," she said,
brushing her wonderful hair, naked except
for the jewelry. "We try to believe."
"You were helpless with joy," he said,
"moaning and weeping." "In the dream," she said,
"we pretend to ourselves that we are touching.
The heart lies to itself because it must."

PUT HER IN THE FIELDS FOR KINDNESS

The door was in the whitewashed eight-foot walls
of the narrow back street common to Greek islands.
Beautiful light and shade in the clear air.
The big iron bolt was on the outside locking
something in. Some days the pounding inside
made the heavy wooden door shudder. Often a voice
screaming. The crazy old woman, people said.
She would hurt the children if they let her out.
Pinch them or scare them, they said.
Sometimes everything was still and I would delay
until I heard the tiny whimper that meant she knew
I was there. Late one afternoon on my way for oil,
the door was broken. She was in the lot opposite
in weeds by the wall, her dress pulled up, pissing.
Like a cow. Able to manage, quiet in the last light.

The massive overhead crane comes
when we wave to it, lets down
its heavy claws and waits tamely
within its power while we hook up
the slabs of three-quarter-inch
steel. Takes away the ponderous
reality when we wave again.
What name do we have for that?
What song is there for its voice?
What is the other face of Yahweh?
The god who made the slug and ferret,
the maggot and shark in his image.
What is the carol for that?
Is it the song of nevertheless,
or of the empire of our heart? We carry
language as our mind, but are we
the dead whale that sinks grandly
for years to reach the bottom of us?

HAVING THE HAVING

For Gianna

I tie knots in the strings of my spirit
to remember. They are not pictures
of what was. Not accounts of dusk
amid the olive trees and that odor.
The walking back was the arriving.
For that there are three knots
and a space and another two
close together. They do not imitate
the inside of her body, nor her clean
mouth. They cannot describe, but they
can prevent remembering it wrong.
The knots recall. The knots
are blazons marking the trail
back to what we own and imperfectly
forget. Back to a bell ringing
far off, and the sweet summer darkening.
All but a little of it blurs and leaks
away, but that little is most of it,
even damaged. Two more knots
and then just straight string.

Are the angels of her bed the angels
who come near me alone in mine?
Are the green trees in her window
the color I see in ripe plums?
If she always sees backward
and upside down without knowing it
what chance do we have? I am haunted
by the feeling that she is saying
melting lords of death, avalanches,
rivers and moments of passing through.
And I am replying, "Yes, yes.
Shoes and pudding."

KUNSTKAMMER

We are resident inside with the machinery,
a glimmering spread throughout the apparatus.
We exist with a wind whispering inside
and our moon flexing. Amid the ducts,
inside the basilica of bones. The flesh
is a neighborhood, but not the life.
Our body is not good at memory, at keeping.
It is the spirit that holds on to our treasure.
The dusk in Italy when the ferry passed Bellagio
and turned across Lake Como in the hush to where
we would land and start up the grassy mountain.
The body keeps so little of the life after
being with her eleven years,
and the mouth not even that much. But the heart
is different. It never forgets
the pine trees with the moon rising behind them
every night. Again and again we put our
sweet ghosts on small paper boats and sailed
them back into their death, each moving slowly
into the dark, disappearing as our hearts
visited and savored, hurt and yearned.

HALLOWEEN

There were a hundred wild people in Allen's
three-story house. He was sitting at a small
table in the kitchen quietly eating something.
Alone, except for Orlovsky's little brother
who was asleep with his face against the wall.
Allen wearing a red skullcap, and a loose bathrobe
over his nakedness. Shoulder-length hair
and a chest-length, oily beard.
No one was within fifteen years of him. Destroyed
like the rest of that clan. His remarkable
talent destroyed. The fine mind grown more
and more simple. Buddhist chants, impoverishing
poems. There are no middle tones in the paintings
of children. Chekhov said he didn't want
the audience to cry, but to see. Allen showing
me his old man's bald scalp. A kind of love.
Aachen is a good copy of a mediocre building.
Architects tried for two thousand years to find
a way to put a dome on a square base.

ELEGY FOR BOB (JEAN MCLEAN)

Only you and I still stand in the snow on Highland Avenue
in Pittsburgh waiting for the blundering iron streetcars
that never came. Only you know how the immense storms
over the Allegheny and Monongahela Rivers were the scale
I wanted. Nobody but you remembers Peabody High School.
You shared my youth in Paris and the hills above Como.
And later, in Seattle. It was you playing the aria from
Don Giovanni over and over, filling the forest of Puget
Sound with the music. You in the front room and me
upstairs with your discarded wife in my bed. The sound
of your loneliness pouring over our happy bodies.
You were with your third wife when I was in Perugia
six months later, but in love with somebody else.
We searched for her in Munich, the snow falling again.
You trying to decide when to kill yourself. All of it
finally bringing us to San Francisco. To the vast
decaying white house. No sound of Mozart coming up
from there. No alleluias in you anymore. No longer
will you waltz under the chandeliers in Paris salons
drunk with champagne and the Greek girl as the others
stand along the mirrored walls. The men watching
with fury, the eyes of the women inscrutable. No one
else speaks the language of those years. No one
remembers you as the Baron. The streetcars have
finished the last run, and I am walking home. Thinking
love is not refuted because it comes to an end.

RÉSUMÉ

Easter on the mountain. The hanging goat roasted
with lemon, pepper and thyme. The American hacks off
the last of the meat, gets out the remaining
handfuls from the spine. Grease up to the elbows,
his face smeared and his heart blooming. The satisfied
farmers watch his fervor with surprise.
When the day begins to cool, he makes his way down
the trails. Down from that holiday energy
to the silence of his real life, where he will
wash in cold water by kerosene light, happy
and alone. A future inch by inch, rock by rock,
by the green wheat and the ripe wheat later.
By basil and dove tower and white doves turning
in the brilliant sky. The ghosts of his other world
crowding around, surrounding him with himself.
Tomato by tomato, canned fish in the daily stew.
He sits outside on the wall of his vineyard
as night rises from the parched earth and the sea
darkens in the distance. Insistent stars and him
singing in the quiet. Flesh of the spirit and soul
of the body. The clarity that does so much damage.

MORE THAN SIXTY

Out of money, so I'm sitting in the shade
of my farmhouse cleaning the lentils
I found in the back of the cupboard.
Listening to the cicada in the fig tree
mix with the cooing doves on the roof.
I look up when I hear a goat hurt far down
the valley and discover the sea
exactly the same blue I used to paint it
with my watercolors as a child.
So what, I think happily. So what!

BY SMALL AND SMALL:
MIDNIGHT TO FOUR A.M.

For eleven years I have regretted it,
regretted that I did not do what
I wanted to do as I sat there those
four hours watching her die. I wanted
to crawl in among the machinery
and hold her in my arms, knowing
the elementary, leftover bit of her
mind would dimly recognize it was me
carrying her to where she was going.

ONCE UPON A TIME

We were young incidentally, stumbling
into joy, he said. The sweetness of
our bodies was natural in the way
the sun came out of the Mediterranean
fresh every morning. We were accidentally
alive. A shape without a form.
We were a music composed of melody,
without chords, played only on
the white keys. We thought excitement
was love, that intensity was a marriage.
We meant no harm, but could see the women
only a little through the ardor and hurry.
We were innocent, he said, baffled when
they let us kiss their tender mouths.
Sometimes they kissed back, even volunteered.

A CLOSE CALL

Dusk and the sea is thus and so. The cat
from two fields away crossing through the grapes.
It is so quiet I can hear the air
in the canebrake. The blond wheat darkens.
The glaze is gone from the bay and the heat lets go.
They have not lit the lamp at the other farm yet
and all at once I feel lonely. What a surprise.
But the air stills, the heat comes back
and I think I am all right again.

THE ROOSTER

They have killed the rooster, thank God,
but it's strange to have my half
of the valley unreported. Without the rooster
it's like my place by the Chinese Elm is not here
each day. As though I'm gone. I touch my face
and get up to make tea, feeling my heart claim
no territory. Like the colorless weeds which fail,
but don't give in. Silent in the world's clamor.
They killed the rooster because he could feel
nothing for the six frumpy hens. Now there is only
the youngster to announce and cover. They are only
aunts to him. Mostly he works on his crowing. And for
a long time the roosters on the other farms would not
answer. But yesterday they started laying
full-throated performances on him. He would come
back, but couldn't get the hang of it. The scorn
and the failing went on until finally one day,
from the other end of the valley, came a deep
voice saying, "For Christ's sake, kid, like this."
And it began. Not bothering to declare parts
of the landscape, but announcing the glory,
the greatness of the sun and moon.
Told of the heavenly hosts, the mysteries,
and the joy. Which were the Huns and which not.
Describing the dominions of wind and song. What was
noble in all things. It was very quiet after that.

FAILING AND FLYING

Everyone forgets that Icarus also flew.
It's the same when love comes to an end,
or the marriage fails and people say
they knew it was a mistake, that everybody
said it would never work. That she was
old enough to know better. But anything
worth doing is worth doing badly.
Like being there by that summer ocean
on the other side of the island while
love was fading out of her, the stars
burning so extravagantly those nights that
anyone could tell you they would never last.
Every morning she was asleep in my bed
like a visitation, the gentleness in her
like antelope standing in the dawn mist.
Each afternoon I watched her coming back
through the hot stony field after swimming,
the sea light behind her and the huge sky
on the other side of that. Listened to her
while we ate lunch. How can they say
the marriage failed? Like the people who
came back from Provence (when it was Provence)
and said it was pretty but the food was greasy.
I believe Icarus was not failing as he fell,
but just coming to the end of his triumph.

BURNING (ANDANTE NON TROPPO)

We are all burning in time, but each is consumed
at his own speed. Each is the product
of his spirit's refraction, of the inflection
of that mind. It is the pace of our living
that makes the world available. Regardless of
the body's lion-wrath or forest waiting, despite
the mind's splendid appetite or the sad power
in our soul's separation from God and women,
it is always our gait of being that decides
how much is seen, what the mystery of us knows,
and what the heart will smell of the landscape
as the Mexican train continues at a dog-trot each
day going north. The grand Italian churches are
covered with detail which is visible at the pace
people walk by. The great modern buildings are
blank because there is no time to see from the car.
A thousand years ago when they built the gardens
of Kyoto, the stones were set in the streams askew.
Whoever went quickly would fall in. When we slow,
the garden can choose what we notice. Can change
our heart. On the wall of a toilet in Rock Springs
years ago there was a dispenser that sold tubes of
cream to numb a man's genitals. Called Linger.

THE OTHER PERFECTION

Nothing here. Rock and fried earth.
Everything destroyed by the fierce light.
Only stones and small fields of
stubborn barley and lentils. No broken
things to repair. Nothing thrown away
or abandoned. If you want a table,
you pay a man to make it. If you find two
feet of barbed wire, you take it home.
You'll need it. The farmers don't laugh.
They go to town to laugh, or to fiestas.
A kind of paradise. Everything itself.
The sea is water. Stones are made of rock.
The sun goes up and goes down. A success
without any enhancement whatsoever.

A BALL OF SOMETHING

Watching the ant walk underwater along
the bottom of my saucepan is painful.
Though he seems in no distress.
He walks at leisure, almost strolling.
Lifts his head twice in the solid outside
and goes on. Until he encounters a bit
of something and acts almost afraid
in struggling to get free. After, he continues,
again at ease. He looks up and pitches forward
into a tight ball. It is not clear whether
that's the end. Perhaps he is doing what
the hedgehog does well. Waiting for someone
to go by whose ankle he can grab
and ask for help. Hoping for pity. But maybe
not. Maybe he lies there curled around a smile,
liberated at last. Dreaming of coming back
as Byron, or maybe the favorite dog.

We have already lived in the real paradise.
Horses in the empty summer street.
Me eating the hot wurst I couldn't afford,
in frozen Munich, tears dropping. We can
remember. A child in the outfield waiting
for the last fly ball of the year. So dark
already it was black against heaven.
The voices trailing away to dinner,
calling faintly in the immense distance.
Standing with my hands open, watching it
curve over and start down, turning white
at the last second. Hands down. Flourishing.

TRUTH

The glare of the Greek sun
on our stone house
is not so white
as the pale moonlight on it.

TRANSGRESSIONS

He thinks about how important the sinning was,
how much his equity was in simply being alive.
Like the sloth. The days and nights wasted,
doing nothing important adding up to
the favorite years. Long hot afternoons
watching ants while the cicadas railed
in the Chinese Elm about the brevity of life.
Indolence so often when no one was watching.
Wasting June mornings with the earth singing
all around. Autumn afternoons doing nothing
but listening to the siren voices of streams
and clouds coaxing him into the sweet happiness
of leaving all of it alone. Using up what
little time we have, relishing our mortality,
waltzing slowly without purpose. Neglecting
the future. Content to let the garden fail
and the house continue on in its usual disorder.
Yes, and coveting his neighbors' wives.
Their clean hair and soft voices. The seraphim
he was sure were in one of the upstairs rooms.
Hesitant occasions of pride, feeling himself feeling.
Waking in the night and lying there. Discovering
the past in the wonderful stillness. The other,
older pride. Watching the ambulance take away
the man whose throat he had crushed. Above all,
his greed. Greed of time, of being. This world,
the pine woods stretching all brown or bare
on either side of the railroad tracks in the winter
twilight. Him feeling the cold, sinfully unshriven.

THE ABANDONED VALLEY

Can you understand being alone so long
you would go out in the middle of the night
and put a bucket into the well
so you could feel something down there
tug at the other end of the rope?

HAPPENING APART FROM WHAT'S
HAPPENING AROUND IT

There is a vividness to eleven years of love
because it is over. A clarity of Greece now
because I live in Manhattan or New England.
If what is happening is part of what's going on
around what's occurring, it is impossible
to know what is truly happening. If love is
part of the passion, part of the fine food
or the villa on the Mediterranean, it is not
clear what the love is. When I was walking
in the mountains with the Japanese man and began
to hear the water, he said, "What is the sound
of the waterfall?" "Silence," he finally told me.
The stillness I did not notice until the sound
of water falling made apparent the silence I had
been hearing long before. I ask myself what
is the sound of women? What is the word for
that still thing I have hunted inside them
for so long? Deep inside the avalanche of joy,
the thing deeper in the dark, and deeper still
in the bed where we are lost. Deeper, deeper
down where a woman's heart is holding its breath,
where something very far away in that body
is becoming something we don't have a name for.

EXCEEDING THE SPIRIT

Beyond what the fires have left of the cathedral
you can see old men standing here and there
in administration buildings looking out
of the fine casements with the glass gone.
Idle and bewildered. The few people who are
in the weed-choked streets below carry things
without purpose, holding fading memories inside
of what the good used to be. Immense ships
rise in the distance, beached and dying.
Starving men crouch in the dirt of the plaza with
a scrap of cloth before them, trying to sell nothing:
one with dead fuses and a burnt-out light bulb,
another with just a heavy bolt and screw
rusted together. One has two Byzantine coins
and a lump of oxidation which has a silver piece
inside stamped with the face of Hermes, but he
doesn't know it. A strange place to look for
what matters, what is worthy. To arrive now
at the wilderness alone and striving harder
for discontent, to need again. Not for salvation.
To go on because there might be something like him.
To visit what is importantly unknown of what is.

MEDITATION ELEVEN:
READING BLAKE AGAIN

I remember that house I'd rented with them.
The laughing and constant talk of love.
The energy of their friends.
And the sounds late at night.
The sound of whipping. Urging and screams.
Like the dead lying to each other.

HOW MUCH OF THAT IS LEFT IN ME?

Yearning inside the rejoicing. The heart's famine
within the spirit's joy. Waking up happy
and practicing discontent. Seeing the poverty
in the perfection, but still hungering
for its strictness. Thinking of
a Greek farmer in the orchard,
the white almond blossoms falling and falling
on him as he struggled with his wooden plow.
I remember the stark and precious winters in Paris.
Just after the war when everyone was poor and cold.
I walked hungry through the vacant streets at night
with the snow falling wordlessly in the dark like petals
on the last of the nineteenth century. Substantiality
seemed so near in the grand empty boulevards,
while the famous bronze bells told of time.
Stripping everything down until being was visible.
The ancient buildings and the Seine,
small stone bridges and regal fountains flourishing
in the emptiness. What fine provender in the want.
What freshness in me amid the loneliness.

'TIS HERE! 'TIS HERE! 'TIS GONE!
(THE NATURE OF PRESENCE)

A white horse, Linda Gregg wrote, is not a horse,
quoting what Hui Shih said twenty-three hundred
years ago. The thing is not its name, is not
the words. The painting of a pipe is not a pipe
regardless of what the title claims. An intelligent
poet in Iowa is frightened because she thinks
we are made of electrons. The Gianna Gelmetti
I loved was a presence ignited in a swarm
of energy, but the ghost living in the mansion
is not the building. Consciousness is not
matter dreaming. If all the stars were added
together they would still not know it's spring.
The silence of the mountain is not our silence.
The sound of the earth will never be *Un bel di*.
We are a contingent occurrence. The white horse
in moonlight is more white than when it stands
in sunlight. And even then it depends on whether
a bell is ringing. The intimate body of the Valerie
I know is not the secret body my friend knows.
The luster of her breasts is conditional:
clothed or not, desired or too familiar.
The fact of them is mediated by morning
or the depth of night when it's pouring down rain.
The reason we cannot enter the same woman
twice is not because the mesh of energy flexes.
It is a mystery separate from both matter
and electrons. It is not why the Linda
looking out over the Aegean is not the Linda
eating melon in Kentucky, nor explains how

the mind lives amid the rain without being
part of it. The dead lady Nogami-san lives now
only in me, in the momentary occasion I am.
Her whiteness in me is the color of pale amber
in winter light.

AMBITION

Having reached the beginning, starting toward
a new ignorance. Places to become,
secrets to live in, sins to achieve.
Maybe South America, perhaps a new woman,
another language to not understand.
Like setting out on a raft over an ocean
of life already well lived.
A two-story failed hotel in the tropics,
hot silence of noon with the sun
straying through the shutters.
Sitting with his poems at a small table,
everybody asleep. Thinking with pleasure,
trailing his hand in the river he will
turn into.

BEING YOUNG BACK THEN

Another beautiful love letter
trying to win her back. Finished,
like each night, just before dawn.
Down the corso Garibaldi to the Piazza
Fortebraccio. Across to the massive
Etruscan gate and up the via
Ulisse Rocchi. To the main square.
Past the cathedral, past the fountain
of Nicola Pisano. And the fine
thirteenth-century town hall.
To the post office so the letter
could get to California in three days.
Then to the palazzo to stand always
for a half hour looking up to where
Gianna was sleeping. Longing for
her and dreaming of the other one.

NOT GETTING CLOSER

Walking in the dark streets of Seoul
under the almost full moon.
Lost for the last two hours.
Finishing a loaf of bread
and worried about the curfew.
I have not spoken for three days
and I am thinking, "Why not just
settle for love? Why not just
settle for love instead?"

ADULTS

The sea lies in its bed wet and naked
in the dark. Half a moon glimmers on it
as though someone had come through
a door with the light behind. The woman thinks
of how they lived in the neighborhood
for years while she belonged to other men.
He moves toward her knowing he is about to
spoil the way they didn't know each other.

SEEN FROM ABOVE

In the end, Hannibal walked out of his city
saying the Romans wanted only him. Why should
his soldiers make love to their swords?
He walked out alone, a small figure in
the great field, his elephants dead at
the bottom of the Alps' crevasses. So might we
go to our Roman death in triumph. Our love
is of marble and large tawny roses,
in the endless harvests of our defeat.
We have slept with death all our lives.
It will grind out its graceless victory,
but we can limp in triumph over the cold
intervening sand.

GETTING CLOSER

The heat's on the bus with us.
The icon in front, the chunk
of raw meat in the rack
on the other side. The boy
languid in the seat under it
rubbing his eyes. Old women
talking almost softly.
Quietly, I look in the bus waiting
next to us and meet the eyes
of a pretty Greek girl.
She looks back steadily.
I drop my eyes and the bus
drives away.

THE MAIL

What the hell are you doing out there
(he writes) in that worn rock valley
with chickens and the donkey and not farming?
And the people around you speaking Greek.
And the only news faint on the Armed
Forces Network. I don't know what to say.
And what about women? he asks. Yes,
I think to myself, what about women?

It started when he was a young man
and went to Italy. He climbed mountains,
wanting to be a poet. But was troubled
by what Dorothy Wordsworth wrote in
her journal about William having worn
himself out searching all day to find
a simile for nightingale. It seemed
a long way from the tug of passion.
He ended up staying in pensioni
where the old women would take up
the children in the middle of the night
to rent the room, carrying them warm
and clinging to the mothers, the babies
making a mewing sound. He began hunting
for the second-rate. The insignificant
ruins, the negligible museums, the back-
country villages with only one pizzeria
and two small bars. The unimproved.

HOMAGE TO WANG WEI

An unfamiliar woman sleeps on the other side
of the bed. Her faint breathing is like a secret
alive inside her. They had known each other
three days in California four years ago. She was
engaged and got married afterwards. Now the winter
is taking down the last of the Massachusetts leaves.
The two o'clock Boston & Maine goes by,
calling out of the night like trombones rejoicing,
leaving him in the silence after. She cried yesterday
when they walked in the woods, but she didn't want
to talk about it. Her suffering will be explained,
but she will be unknown nevertheless. Whatever happens,
he will not find her. Despite the tumult and trespass
they might achieve in the wilderness of their bodies
and the voices of the heart clamoring, they will still
be a mystery each to the other, and to themselves.

THE BUTTERNUT TREE AT FORT JUNIPER

I called the tree a butternut (which I don't think
it is) so I could talk about how different
the trees are around me here in the rain.
It reminds me how mutable language is. Keats
would leave blank places in his drafts to hold on
to his passion, spaces for the right words to come.
We use them sideways. The way we automatically
add bits of shape to hold on to the dissolving dreams.
So many of the words are for meanwhile. We say,
"I love you" while we search for language
that can be heard. Which allows us to talk
about how the aspens over there tremble
in the smallest shower, while the tree over by
the window here gathers the raindrops and lets them
go in bunches. The way my heart carols sometimes,
and other times yearns. Sometimes is quiet
and other times is powerfully quiet.

TRY

ou sonofabitch, it's bad enough
embarrass myself working so hard
it right even a little,
    that little grudging and awkward.
But it's afterwards I resent, when
the sweet sure should hold me like
a trout in the bright summer stream.
There should be at least briefly
access to your glamour and tenderness.
But there's always this same old
dissatisfaction instead.

HOMESTEADING

It would be easy if the spirit
was reasonable, was old.
But there is a stubborn gladness.
Summer air idling in the elms.
Silence hunting in the towering
storms of heaven. Thirty-two
swans in a København dusk.
The swan bleeding to death
slowly in a Greek kitchen.
A man leaves the makeshift
restaurant plotting his improvidence.
Something voiceless flies lovely
over an empty landscape.
He wanders on the way
to whoever he will become.
Passion leaves us single and safe.
The other fervor leaves us
at risk, in love, and alone.
Married sometimes forever.

THE SWEET TASTE OF THE NIGHT

When I woke up my head was saying, "The world
will pardon my mush, but I've got a crush"
and I went outside. The wind was gone.
The last of the moon was just up and the stars
brighter even than usual. A freighter
in the distance was turning into the bay,
all lit up. The valley was so still I could
hear the engine. The dogs quiet, worn out barking
all week at the full moon. Their ease in failure.
The ship came out the other side of the hill
and blew its horn softly for the harbor.
Waking a rooster on the mountain. It went
behind the second hill and I started back inside
the farmhouse. "All the day and night time,
hear me cry. The world will pardon my emotion,"
I sang from my bed, up into the dark, my voice
unfamiliar after not speaking for days.
Thinking of Linda, but singing to something else.

HONOR

All honor at a distance is punctilio.
One dies dutifully by a code
which applies to nothing recognizable.
It is like the perfect grace of our
contessa who has been mad and foul
for the last thirty years.

TRYING TO WRITE POETRY

There is a wren sitting in the branches
of my spirit and it chooses not to sing.
It is listening to learn its song.
Sits in the Palladian light trying to decide
what it will sing when it is time to sing.
Tra la, tra la, the other birds sing
in the morning, and silently when the snow
is slowly falling just before evening.
Knowing that passion is not a color
not confused by energy. The bird will sing
about summer having its affair with Italy.
Is frightened of classical singing.
Will sing happily of the color fruits are
in the cool dark, the wetness inside
overripe peaches, the smell of melons
and the briars that come with berries.
When the sun falls into silence,
the two birds will sing. Back and forth,
making a whole. Silence answering silence.
Song answering song. Gone and gone.
Gone somewhere. Gone nowhere.

A KIND OF COURAGE

The girl shepherd on the farm beyond has been
taken from school now she is twelve, and her life is over.
I got my genius brother a summer job in the mills
and he stayed all his life. I lived with a woman four
years who went crazy later, escaped from the hospital,
hitchhiked across America terrified and in the snow
without a coat. Was raped by most men who gave her
a ride. I crank my heart even so and it turns over.
Ranges high in the sun over continents and eruptions
of mortality, through winds and immensities of rain
falling for miles. Until all the world is overcome
by what goes up and up in us, singing and dancing
and throwing down flowers nevertheless.

HAPPILY PLANTING THE BEANS TOO EARLY

I waited until the sun was going down
to plant the bean seedlings. I was
beginning on the peas when the phone rang.
It was a long conversation about what
living this way in the woods might
be doing to me. It was dark by the time
I finished. Made tuna fish sandwiches
and read the second half of a novel.
Found myself out in the April moonlight
putting the rest of the pea shoots into
the soft earth. It was after midnight.
There was a bird calling intermittently
and I could hear the stream down below.
She was probably right about me getting
strange. After all, Bashō and Tolstoy
at the end were at least going somewhere.

WHAT TO WANT

The room was like getting married.
A landfall and the setting forth.
A dearness and vessel. A small room
eight by twelve, filled by the narrow iron bed.
Six stories up, under the roof
and no elevator. A maid's room long ago.
In the old quarter, on the other hill
with the famous city stretched out
below. His window like an ocean.
The great bells of the cathedral counting
the hours all night while everyone slept.
After two years, he had come to
the beginning. Past the villa at Como,
past the police moving him from jail
to jail to hide him from the embassy.
His first woman gone back to Manhattan,
the friends gone back to weddings
or graduate school. He was finally alone.
Without money. A wind blowing through
where much of him used to be. No longer
the habit of himself. The blinding intensity
giving way to presence. The budding
amid the random passion. Mortality like
a cello inside him. Like rain in the dark.
Sin a promise. What interested him
most was who he was about to become.

BRING IN THE GODS

Bring in the gods I say, and he goes out. When he comes
back and I know they are with him, I say, Put tables in front
of them so they may be seated, and food upon the tables
so they may eat. When they have eaten, I ask which of them
will question me. Let him hold up his hand, I say.
The one on the left raises his hand and I tell him to ask.
Where are you now, he says. I stand on top of myself, I hear
myself answer. I stand on myself like a hilltop and my life
is spread before me. Does it surprise you, he asks. I explain
that in our youth and for a long time after our youth we cannot
see our lives. Because we are inside of that. Because we can
see no shape to it since we have nothing to compare it to.
We have not seen it grow and change because we are too close.
We don't know the names of things that would bind them to us,
so we cannot feed on them. One near the middle asks why not.
Because we don't have the knack for eating what we are living.
Why is that? she asks. Because we are too much in a hurry.
Where are you now? the one on the left says. With the ghosts.
I am with Gianna those two years in Perugia. Meeting secretly
in the thirteenth-century alleys of stone. Walking in the fields
through the spring light, she well dressed and walking in heels
over the plowed land. We are just outside the city walls
hidden under the thorny blackberry bushes and her breasts naked.
I am with her those many twilights in the olive orchards,
holding the heart of her as she whimpers. Now where are you?
he says. I am with Linda those years and years. In American
cities, in København, on Greek islands season after season.
Lindos and Monolithos and the other places. I am with Michiko
for eleven years, East and West, holding her clear in my mind
the way a native can hold all of his village at one moment.
Where are you now? he says. I am standing on myself the way
a bird sits in her nest, with the babies half asleep underneath

and the world all leaves and morning air. What do you want?
a blonde one asks. To keep what I already have, I say. You ask
too much, he says sternly. Then you are at peace, she says.
I am not at peace, I tell her. I want to fail. I am hungry
for what I am becoming. What will you do? she asks. I will
continue north, carrying the past in my arms, flying into winter.

THE NEGLIGIBLE

I lie in bed listening to it sing
in the dark about the sweetness
of brief love and the perfection of loves
that might have been. The spirit cherishes
the disregarded. It is because the body continues
to fail at remembering the smell of Michiko
that her body is so clear in me after all this time.
There is a special pleasure in remembering the shine
on her spoon merging with faint sounds
in the distance of her rising from the bathwater.

THE LOST HOTELS OF PARIS

The Lord gives everything and charges
by taking it back. What a bargain.
Like being young for a while. We are
allowed to visit hearts of women,
to go into their bodies so we feel
no longer alone. We are permitted
romantic love with its bounty and half-life
of two years. It is right to mourn
for the small hotels of Paris that used to be
when we used to be. My mansard looking
down on Notre Dame every morning is gone,
and me listening to the bell at night.
Venice is no more. The best Greek islands
have drowned in acceleration. But it's the having
not the keeping that is the treasure.
Ginsberg came to my house one afternoon
and said he was giving up poetry
because it told lies, that language distorts.
I agreed, but asked what we have
that gets it right even that much.
We look up at the stars and they are
not there. We see the memory
of when they were, once upon a time.
And that too is more than enough.

FEATHERS OR LEAD

Him, she said, and him. They put us in the second car
and followed her back to the villa. Our fear slowly
faded during the weeks. Everyone was kind but busy.
We could go anywhere on the first floor
and on the grounds this side of the fence.
They decided on me and sent the other boy away.
Before I had only glimpsed her at the upper windows.
Now we ate together at opposite ends of the table.
Candlelight eased her age, but not her guilt.
Once she said the world was an astonishing animal:
light was its spirit and noise was its mind.
That it was composed to feed on honor, but did not.
Another time she warned me about walking on the lawns
at night. Told me of heavy birds that flew after dark
croaking, "Feathers or lead, stone or fire?"
Mounting people who gave the wrong answer and riding
them like horses across the whole county, beating them
with their powerful wings. We would play cards
silently on rainy days, and have sardine sandwiches
at four in the morning, taking turns reading aloud
from Tolstoy. "What need do we have for consulates?"
she said once before going upstairs, the grand room
beginning to fill with the dawn. "Why insist
on nature? A flower must be red or white, but we
can be anything. Our victories are difficult
because the triumph is not in possessing excellence.
It is found in reluctance." Month after month
we lived like that. And with me telling her
what it was like out there among the living.
She was steadily failing, like a Palladian palace

coming apart gracefully. The last morning she stood
by the tall windows. "I will not give you my blessing,"
she said, "and I refuse you also my reasons. Who are you,
who is anyone to make me just?" When they came for her,
she smiled at me and said, "At last."

WHAT PLENTY

Hitting each other. Backing up
and hitting each other again
in the loud silence of the stars
and the roar of their headlights.
Trying to force feeling and squeezing
out pain. Eden built of iron and grit.
Arcades fashioned entirely of guilt.
Paradise of loss, of lipsticked nipples,
lying to children about the soul.
Dead women stuffed with flowers.
Abandoned cabs in empty streets
not listening to the red lights,
yellow nor green.

THE GARDEN

We come from a deep forest of years
into a valley of an unknown country
called loneliness. Without horse or dog,
the heavens bottomless overhead.
We are like Marco Polo who came back
with jewels hidden in the seams of his ragged clothes.
A sweet sadness, a tough happiness.
This beginner cobbles together a kind of house
and makes lentil soup there night
after night. Sits on the great stone
that is a threshold, smelling pine trees
in the hot darkness. When the moon rises
between the tall trunks, he sings without
talent but with pleasure. Then goes inside
to make courtesy with his dear ghosts.
In the morning, he watches the two nuthatches,
the pair of finches with their new son.
And the chickadees. There are chipmunks
in the afternoon finding seeds between
his fingers with their exquisite hands.
He visits his misbegotten garden where
the mint and chives flourish alongside
the few stunted tomatoes and eggplants.
They are scarce because of ignorance.
He wonders all the time where
he has arrived, why so much has been
allowed him (even rain on the leaves
of sugar maples), and why there is
even now so much to come.

MUSIC IS IN THE PIANO
ONLY WHEN IT IS PLAYED

We are not one with this world. We are not
the complexity our body is, nor the summer air
idling in the big maple without purpose.
We are a shape the wind makes in these leaves
as it passes through. We are not the wood
any more than the fire, but the heat which is a marriage
between the two. We are certainly not the lake
nor the fish in it, but the something that is
pleased by them. We are the stillness when
a mighty Mediterranean noon subtracts even the voices
of insects by the broken farmhouse. We are evident
when the orchestra plays, and yet are not part
of the strings or brass. Like the song that exists
only in the singing, and is not the singer.
God does not live among the church bells,
but is briefly resident there. We are occasional
like that. A lifetime of easy happiness mixed
with pain and loss, trying always to name and hold
on to the enterprise underway in our chest.
Reality is not what we marry as a feeling. It is what
walks up the dirt path, through the excessive heat
and giant sky, the sea stretching away.
He continues past the nunnery to the old villa
where he will sit on the terrace with her, their sides
touching. In the quiet that is the music of that place,
which is the difference between silence and windlessness.

WINNING ON THE BLACK

The silence is so complete he can hear
the whispers inside him. Mostly names
of women. Women gone or dead. The ones
we loved so easily. What is it, he wonders,
that we had then and don't have now,
that we once were and are no longer.
It seemed natural to be alive back then.
Soon there will be only the raccoon's
tracks in the snow down by the river.

The old women in black at early Mass in winter
are a problem for him. He could tell by their eyes
they have seen Christ. They make the kernel
of his being and the clarity around it
seem meager, as though he needs girders
to hold up his unusable soul. But he chooses
against the Lord. He will not abandon his life.
Not his childhood, not the ninety-two bridges
across the two rivers of his youth. Nor the mills
along the banks where he became a young man
as he worked. The mills are eaten away, and eaten
again by the sun and its rusting. He needs them
even though they are gone, to measure against.
The silver is worn down to the brass underneath
and is the better for it. He will gauge
by the smell of concrete sidewalks after night rain.
He is like an old ferry dragged onto the shore,
a home in its smashed grandeur, with the giant beams
and joists. Like a wooden ocean out of control.
A beached heart. A cauldron of cooling melt.

THE FRIENDSHIP INSIDE US

Why the mouth? Why is it the mouth we put to mouth
at the final moments? Why not the famous groin?
Because the groin is far away.
The mouth is close up against the spirit.
We couple desperately all night before setting out
for years in prison. But that is the body's goodbye.
We kiss the person we love last thing before
the coffin is shut, because it is our being
touching the unknown. A kiss is the frontier in us.
It is where the courting becomes the courtship,
where the dancing ends and the dance begins.
The mouth is our chief access to the intimacy
in which she may reside. Her mouth is the porch
of the brain. The forecourt of the heart.
The way to the mystery enthroned. Where we meet
momentarily amid the seraphim and the powers.

A THANKSGIVING DANCE

His spirit dances the long ago, and later.
Starlight on a country road in worn-out
western Pennsylvania. The smell of weeds
and rusting iron. And gladness.
His spirit welcomes the Italian New Year's
in a hill town filled with the music
of glass crashing everywhere in the cobbled
streets. Champagne and the first kisses.
Too shy to look at each other and no language
between them. He dances alone, the dance
of after that. Now they sit amid the heavy
Roman sunlight and talk of the people
they are married to now. He secretly
dances the waltz she was in her astonishing
beauty, drinking wine and laughing, the window
behind her filled with winter rain.

HORSES AT MIDNIGHT WITHOUT A MOON

Our heart wanders lost in the dark woods.
Our dream wrestles in the castle of doubt.
But there's music in us. Hope is pushed down
but the angel flies up again taking us with her.
The summer mornings begin inch by inch
while we sleep, and walk with us later
as long-legged beauty through
the dirty streets. It is no surprise
that danger and suffering surround us.
What astonishes is the singing.
We know the horses are there in the dark
meadow because we can smell them,
can hear them breathing.
Our spirit persists like a man struggling
through the frozen valley
who suddenly smells flowers
and realizes the snow is melting
out of sight on top of the mountain,
knows that spring has begun.

IMMACULATE

For Michiko

The brain is dead and the body is
no longer infected by the spirit.
Now it is just machines talking
to the machine. Helping it back
to its old, pure journey.

MOREOVER

We are given the trees so we can know
what God looks like. And rivers
so we might understand Him. We are allowed
women so we can get into bed with the Lord,
however partial and momentary that is.
The passion, and then we are single again
while the dark goes on. He lived
in the Massachusetts woods for two years.
Went out naked among the summer pines
at midnight when the moon would allow it.
He watched the aspens when the afternoon breeze
was at them. And listened to rain
on the butternut tree near his window.
But when he finally left, they did not care.
The difficult garden he was midwife to
was indifferent. The eight wild birds
he fed through both winters, when the snow
was starving them, forgot him immediately.
And the three women he ate of and entered
utterly then and before, who were his New World
as immensity and landfall, are now only friends
or dead. What we are given is taken away,
but we manage to keep it secretly.
We lose everything, but make harvest
of the consequence it was to us. Memory
builds this kingdom from the fragments
and approximation. We are gleaners who fill
the barn for the winter that comes on.

A KIND OF DECORUM

It is burden enough that death lies on all sides,
that your old kimono is still locked in my closet.
Now I wonder what would happen if my life did
catch on fire again. Would I break in half,
part of me a storm and part like ice in a silver bowl?
I lie awake remembering the birds of Kyoto
calling *No No*, unh unh. *No No*, unh unh. And you
saying yes all night. You said yes when I woke you
again in the dawn. And even disgracefully
at lunchtime. Until all the men at the small inn
roamed about, hoping to see whoever that voice was.
The Buddha tells us we should clear every obstacle
out of the way. "If you meet your mother in the path,
kill her. If the Buddha gets in the way, kill him."
But my spirit sings like the perishing cicadas
while I sit in the back yard hitting an old pot.

A WALK BLOSSOMING

The spirit opens as life closes down.
Tries to frame the size of whatever God is.
Finds that dying makes us visible.
Realizes we must get to the loin of that
before time is over. The part of which
we are the wall around. Not the good or evil,
neither death nor afterlife but the importance
of what we contain meanwhile. (He walks along
remembering, biting into beauty,
the heart eating into the naked spirit.)
The body is a major nation, the mind is a gift.
Together they define substantiality.
The spirit can know the Lord as a flavor
rather than power. The soul is ambitious
for what is invisible. Hungers for a sacrament
that is both spirit and flesh. And neither.

FARMING IN SECRET

They piled the bound angels with the barley
in the threshing ring and drove the cow
and donkeys over them all day. Threw the mix
into the wind from the sea to separate
the blond grain from the gold of what
had been. It burned in the luminous air.
When the night came, the mound of chaff
was almost higher than the farmhouse. But there
were only eight sacks of the other.

DECEMBER NINTH, 1960

Walked around Bologna at three in the morning.
Beautiful, arcaded, deserted piazza and winter rain.
Got the train at five of four. Slept badly
in a hot compartment, curled up on my half
of the seat. No real dawn. Beginning to see
a little into the mist. The looming mountain
brindled with snow. The higher pines crusted.
Oyster-white behind them. The train running along
a river between the hills. Mostly apple orchards
with occasionally pale apples still near the top.
Also vineyards. No feeling of Italy here.
No sense of the Umbrian peasants farming
with their white ocean. A tractor instead
putting out compost near an orchard with rotten
red squash gourds. Later another man standing
in the river with a long-handled net, looking
steadily down. Then the commuter line between
Bolzano and Merano. Changing pants on the toilet.
Checked my bag in the station and walked
to the center of the town. Hotels everywhere.
Mountain scenery in the summer, skiing in winter.
Went into the CIT and asked about Pound. (Because
the address had been left at home in Perugia.)
They said he was not there anymore. Went to
the tourist office. Herr Herschel said, yes, Pound
was still there. I came out chuckling, as though
I had been sly. Then, waiting for the first bus
to Tirolo. It leaves at ten-thirty. It's supposed
to be a half hour's walk from there.

NOT THE HAPPINESS BUT
THE CONSEQUENCE OF HAPPINESS

He wakes up in the silence of the winter woods,
the silence of birds not singing, knowing he will
not hear his voice all day. He remembers what
the brown owl sounded like while he was sleeping.
The man wakes in the frigid morning thinking
about women. Not with desire so much as with a sense
of what is not. The January silence is the sound
of his feet in the snow, a squirrel scolding,
or the scraping calls of a single blue jay.
Something of him dances there, apart and gravely mute.
Many days in the woods he wonders what it is
that he has for so long hunted down. We go hand
in hand, he thinks, into the dark pleasure,
but we are rewarded alone, just as we are married
into aloneness. He walks the paths doing the strange
mathematics of the brain, multiplying the spirit.
He thinks of caressing her feet as she kept dying.
For the last four hours, watching her gradually stop
as the hospital slept. Remembers the stunning
coldness of her head when he kissed her just after.
There is light or more light, darkness and less darkness.
It is, he decides, a quality without definition.
How strange to discover that one lives with the heart
as one lives with a wife. Even after many years,
nobody knows what she is like. The heart has
a life of its own. It gets free of us, escapes,
is ambitiously unfaithful. Dies out unaccountably
after eight years, blooms unnecessarily and too late.
Like the arbitrary silence in the white woods,
leaving tracks in the snow he cannot recognize.

INFIDELITY

She is never dead when he meets her.
They eat noodles for breakfast as usual.
For eleven years he thought it was the river
at the bottom of his mind dreaming.
Now he knows she is living inside him,
as the wind is sometimes visible
in the trees. As the roses and rhubarb
are in the garden and then not.
Her ashes are by the sea in Kamakura.
Her face and hair and sweet body still
in the old villa on a mountain where
she lived the whole summer. They slept
on the floor for eleven years.
But now she comes less and less.

THE REINVENTION OF HAPPINESS

I remember how I'd lie on my roof
listening to the fat violinist
below in the sleeping village
play Schubert so badly, so well.

LOOKING AT PITTSBURGH FROM PARIS

The boat of his heart is tethered to the ancient
stone bridges. Beached on the Pacific hills with
thick evening fog flooding whitely over the ridge.
Running in front of the Provençal summer. Drowned
as a secret under the broad Monongahela River.
Forever richly laden with Oak Street and Umbria.
"There be monsters," they warn in the blank spaces
of the old maps. But the real danger is the ocean's
insufficiency, the senseless repetition throughout
the empty waters. Calm and storms and calm again.
Too impoverished for the human. We come to know
ourselves as immense continents and archipelagoes
of endless bounty. He waits now in the hold
of a wooden ship. Becalmed, maybe standing to.
Bobbing, rocking softly. The cargo of ghosts
and angels all around. The wraiths, surprisingly,
singing with the clear voices of young boys.
The angels clapping the rhythm. As he watches
for morning, for the dark to give way and show
his landfall, the new country, his native land.

"MY EYES ADORED YOU"

For Kerry O'Keefe

She came into his life like arriving halfway
through a novel, with bits of two earlier lives
snagged in her. She was the daughter of
a deputy attorney general. And when
that crashed she tried singing and got married.
Now she is in trouble again, leaving soup
on his porch before really knowing him.
Saying she heard he had a bad cold, and besides
it was a tough winter. (It was like
his first wife who went to the department store
and bought a brass bed, getting a salesman
his size to lie down so she could see if it fit.
When she still knew him only at a distance.)
But when people grow up, they should know better.
You can't call it romance when she already had
two children. He had decided never again to get
involved with love. Now everything
has gone wrong. She doesn't just sing softly
up to his window. You can see them in the dark
upstairs, him singing badly and her not minding.

Gradually we realize what is felt is not so important
(however lovely or cruel) as what the feeling contains.
Not what happens to us in childhood, but what was
inside what happened. Ken Kesey sitting in the woods,
beyond his fence of whitewashed motorcycles, said when
he was writing on acid he was not writing about it.
He used what he wrote as blazes to find his way back
to what he knew then. Poetry registers
feelings, delights and passion, but the best searches
out what is beyond pleasure, is outside process.
Not the passion so much as what the fervor can be
an ingress to. Poetry fishes us to find a world
part by part, as the photograph interrupts the flux
to give us time to see each thing separate and enough.
The poem chooses part of our endless flowing forward
to know its merit with attention.

DUENDE

I can't remember her name.
It's not as though I've been in bed
with that many women.
The truth is I can't even remember
her face. I kind of know how strong
her thighs were, and her beauty.
But what I won't forget
is the way she tore open
the barbecued chicken with her hands,
and wiped the grease on her breasts.

THE GOOD LIFE

When he wakes up, a weak sun is just rising
over the side of the valley. It is eight
degrees below zero in the house.
He builds a fire and makes tea. Puts out seeds
for the birds and examines the tracks
in fresh snow, still trying to learn
what lives here. He is writing a poem
when his friend calls. She asks what
he plans to do today. To write some
letters, he tells her (because he is falling
behind in his project of writing one
every day for a month).
She tells him how many letters famous poets
write each day. Says she doesn't mean
that as criticism. After they hang up,
he stands looking at the unanswered mail
heaped high on the table. Gets back
in bed and starts reworking his poem.

FLAT HEDGEHOGS

For Isaiah Berlin

When the hedgehogs here at night
see a car and its fierce lights
coming at them, they do the one
big thing they know.

PROSPERO LISTENING TO THE NIGHT

The intricate vast process has produced
a singularity which lies in darkness
hearing the small owls, a donkey snorting
in the barley field, and frogs down near
the cove. What he is listening to is
the muteness of the dog at each farm
in the valley. Their silence means no
lover is abroad nor any vagrant looking
for where to sleep. But there is a young
man, very still, under the heavy grapes
in another part of Heaven. There are still
women hoping behind the dark windows
of farmhouses. Like he can hear himself not
hearing Verdi. What else don't the dogs know?

When the angels found him sitting in the half light
of his kerosene lamp eating lentils, his eyes widened.
But all he said was could he leave a note. The one
wearing black looked at the one in red who shrugged,
so he began writing, desperately. Wadded the message
into an envelope and wrote *Anna* on the front. Quickly
began another, shoulders hunched, afraid of them.
Finished and wrote *Pimpaporn* on it. Began a third
one and the heavy angel growled. "I have Schubert,"
the man offered, turning on the tape. The one in black
said quietly that at least he didn't say "So soon!"
When the ink ran out, the man whimpered and struggled
to the table piled with books and drafts. He finished
again and scrawled *Suzanne* across it. The one in red
growled again and the man said he would put on his shoes.
When they took him out into the smell of dry vetch
and the ocean, he began to hold back, pleading:
"I didn't put the addresses! I don't want them to think
I forgot." "It doesn't matter," the better angel said,
"they have been dead for years."

THE LOST WORLD

Think what it was like, he said. Peggy Lee and Goodman
all the time. Carl Ravazza making me crazy
with "Vieni Su" from a ballroom in New Jersey
every night, the radio filling my dark room
in Pittsburgh with naked-shouldered women
in black gowns. Helen Forrest and Helen O'Connell,
and later the young Sarah Vaughan out of Chicago
from midnight until two. Think of being fifteen
in the middle of leafy June when Sinatra and Ray
Eberle both had number one records of "Fools Rush In."
Somebody singing "Tenderly" and somebody doing
"This Love of Mine." Helplessly adolescent while
the sound of romance was constantly everywhere.
All day long out of windows along the street.
Sinatra with "Close to You." And all the bands. Artie
Shaw with "Green Eyes" and whoever was always playing
"Begin the Beguine." Me desperate because I wouldn't
get there in time. Who can blame me for my heart?
What choice did I have? Harry James with "Sleepy
Lagoon." Imagine, on a summer night, "Sleepy Lagoon"!

MAYBE VERY HAPPY

After she died he was seized
by a great curiosity about what
it was like for her. Not that he
doubted how much she loved him.
But he knew there must have been
some things she had not liked.
So he went to her closest friend
and asked what she complained of.
"It's all right," he had to keep
saying, "I really won't mind."
Until the friend finally gave in.
"She said sometimes you made a noise
drinking your tea if it was very hot."

THE MANGER OF INCIDENTALS

We are surrounded by the absurd excess of the universe.
By meaningless bulk, vastness without size,
power without consequence. The stubborn iteration
that is present without being felt.
Nothing the spirit can marry. Merely phenomenon
and its physics. An endless, endless of going on.
No habitat where the brain can recognize itself.
No pertinence for the heart. Helpless duplication.
The horror of none of it being alive.
No red squirrels, no flowers, not even weed.
Nothing that knows what season it is.
The stars uninflected by awareness.
Miming without implication. We alone see the iris
in front of the cabin reach its perfection
and quickly perish. The lamb is born into happiness
and is eaten for Easter. We are blessed
with powerful love and it goes away. We can mourn.
We live the strangeness of being momentary,
and still we are exalted by being temporary.
The grand Italy of meanwhile. It is the fact of being brief,
being small and slight that is the source of our beauty.
We are a singularity that makes music out of noise
because we must hurry. We make a harvest of loneliness
and desiring in the blank wasteland of the cosmos.

I woke up every morning on the fourth floor,
in the two-hundred-year-old walls made
of plaster and river grass. I would leave
the woman and walk across beautiful København
to the island of Amager. To my small room
in the leftover Nazi barracks that looked out
on a swamp. Most of the time it was winter.
I would light my hydrant-size iron stove
and set a pot on top, putting in hamburger
and vegetables while the water was getting hot.
Starting to type with numb hands. The book
I planned to write in two weeks for a thousand
dollars already a week behind (and threatening
to get beyond a month). Out of money and no
prospects. Then the lovely smell of soup
and the room snug. I would type all day
and late into the night. Until the soup
was finished. Then I would start back across
the frozen city, crunching over the moats,
loud in the silence. The stars brilliant.
Focused on her waiting for me, ready to fry
sausages at two in the morning. Me thinking idly
of the ancient Chinese poet writing in his
poverty, "Ah, is this not happiness."

BURMA

Used, misled, cheated. Our time always shortening.
What we cherish always temporary. What we love
is, sooner or later, changed. But for a while we can
visit our other life. Can rejoice in its being there
in its absence. Giving thanks for what we are allowed
to think about it, grateful for it even as it wanes.
For knowing it is there. The way women on rainy days
sometimes go into the bedroom to cry about losing
the first man they loved. The way a man remembers the young
woman at an upstairs window looking out he saw once,
for a moment, as he drove through a sleeping village.
Or the brightness in the memory of the failed hotel
where the waiters in their immaculate white uniforms
were barefoot. The elegant dining room silent except for
the sound of rain falling in the tin buckets. And
the whispering of giant overhead fans with broken
blades as they turned in the heat. There was the scraping
sound in the piles of dead leaves on the lavish veranda.
And occasionally the bright sound of broken glass.
All of it a blessing. The being there. Being alive then.
Like a giant bell ringing long after you can't hear it.

WHAT I'VE GOT

After twenty hours in bed with no food, I decided
I should have at least tea. Got up to light the lamp,
but the sweating and shivering started again
and I staggered backwards across the room. Slammed
against the stone wall. Came to with blood on my head
and couldn't figure out which way the bed was.
Crawled around searching for the matches but gave up,
remembering there was one left in a box by the stove.
It flared and went out. "Exaggerated," I said
and groped back toward my desk, feeling for the matches
with barefoot geisha steps. Began to shake and moan,
my teeth chattering like the hero did in the old movie
when his malaria returned. I smiled but was worried.
No telephone and nobody going by out there in the field
I could call to. And God knows what I had. Realized
I was on all fours again. Interesting, something said
as I dragged myself onto the bed. Interesting?
another part said. Interesting! For Christ's sake!

TROUBLE

That is what the Odyssey means.
Love can leave you nowhere in New Mexico
raising peacocks for the rest of your life.
The seriously happy heart is a problem.
Not the easy excitement, but summer
in the Mediterranean mixed with
the rain and bitter cold of February
on the Riviera, everything on fire
in the violent winds. The pregnant heart
is driven to hopes that are the wrong
size for this world. Love is always
disturbing in the heavenly kingdom.
Eden cannot manage so much ambition.
The kids ran from all over the piazza
yelling and pointing and jeering
at the young Saint Chrysostom
standing dazed in the church doorway
with the shining around his mouth
where the Madonna had kissed him.

IN THE BEGINNING

In the morning when Eve and Adam
woke to snow and their minds,
they set out in marvelous clothes
hand in hand under the trees.

Endlessly precision met them,
until they went grinning in time
with no word for their close
escape from that warm monotony.

MÉTIER

The Greek fishermen do not
play on the beach and I don't
write funny poems.

YELAPA

Having swum in the jungle pool
under the waterfall and struggled
down again through the wattle huts,
we still had three hours to wait
before the boat would go back.
The only foreigners had a gallery.
She was British and naked in her halter.
He also was standard, with his stubble
and drunken talk of sex at ten
in the morning. Telling us loudly
how she stayed with him because
of his three hundred a month. She waded
through their old hatred picking up
the sketches as each in turn blew down
in the wind running before the storm.

A TASTE FOR GRIT AND WHATEVER

More and more it is the incidental that makes
him yearn, and he worries about that.
Why should the single railroad tracks
curving away into the bare December trees
and no houses matter? And why is it
the defeated he trusts? Is it because
Pittsburgh is still tangled in him that he
has the picture on his wall of God's head
torn apart by jungle roots? Maybe
growing up in that brutal city left him
with a taste for grit and whatever it was
he saw in the titanic rusting steel mills.
It might be the reason he finally moved out
of Paris. Perhaps it is the scale
of those long-ago winters that makes him
restless when people laugh a lot.
Why the erotic matters so much. Not as
pleasure but a way to get to something darker.
Hunting down the soul, searching out the iron
of Heaven when the work is getting done.

MAYBE SHE IS HERE

She might be here secretly.
On her hands and knees
with her head down a bit
tilted to peer around the doorjamb
in the morning, watching me
before I wake up.
Only her face showing
and her shoulders. In a slip,
her skin honey against the simple
white of two thin straps
and the worked edge of the bodice.
With her right hand a little visible.

THE DANCE
MOST OF ALL

[2009]

EVERYWHERE AND FOREVER

It pleases him that the villa is on a mountain
flayed bare by the great sun. All around
are a thousand stone walls in ruin. He likes knowing
the house was built by the king's telegrapher.
"To write at a distance." He keeps the gate closed
with a massive hasp and chain. The weeds inside
are breast-high around the overgrown rosebushes
and two plum trees. Beyond that, broad stairs
rise to a handsome terrace and the fine house
with its tall windows. He has excavated most
of the courtyard in back. It's there they
spent their perfect days under a diseased
grape arbor and the flowering jasmine. There is
a faint sound of water from the pool over by
the pomegranate tree with its exaggerated fruit.
The basin is no longer choked by the leaves
accumulated in the twelve years of vacancy.
He has come to the right place at the right time.
The blue Aegean is far down, and the slow ships
far out. Doves fly without meaning overhead.
He and the Japanese lady go out the back gate
and up the stream stone by stone, bushes on each side
heavy with moths. They come out under big plane trees.
There is a dirt path from there to a nunnery.
She says goodbye and he starts down to the village
at the bottom where he will get their food for a week.
The sky is vast overhead. Neither of them knows
she is dying. He thinks of their eleven years together.
Realizes they used up all that particular time
everywhere in the cosmos, and forever.

PAINTING ON PLATO'S WALL

The shadows behind people walking
in the bright piazza are not merely
gaps in the sunlight. Just as goodness
is not the absence of badness.
Goodness is a triumph. And so it is
with love. Love is not the part
we are born with that flowers
a little and then wanes as we
grow up. We cobble love together
from this and those of our machinery
until there is suddenly an apparition
that never existed before. There it is,
unaccountable. The woman and our
desire are somehow turned into
brandy by Athena's tiny owl filling
the darkness around an old villa
on the mountain with its plaintive
mewing. As a man might be
turned into someone else while
living kind of happy up there
with the lady's gentle dying.

ALYOSHA

The sound of women hidden
among the lemon trees. A sweetness
that can live with the mind, a family
that does not wear away. He will let
twenty lives pass and choose the twenty-
first. He longs to live married to
slowness. He lives now with the lambs
the minute they are being born,
lives with their perfection as they
blunder around right away in pure innocence.
He watches them go up the mountain
each morning with the twelve-year-old
nearly child. Living with his faith
as he watches them eaten at Easter
to celebrate Christ. He is not innocent.
He knows the shepherdess will be given
to the awful man who lives at the farm
closest to him. He blesses all of it
as he mourns and the white doves soar
silently in the perfect blue sky.

WINTER IN THE NIGHT FIELDS

I was getting water tonight
off guard when I saw the moon
in my bucket and was tempted
by those Chinese poets
and their immaculate pain.

Love is like a garden in the heart, he said.
They asked him what he meant by garden.
He explained about gardens. "In the cities,"
he said, "there are places walled off where color
and decorum are magnified into a civilization.
Like a beautiful woman," he said. How like
a woman, they asked. He remembered their wives
and said garden was just a figure of speech,
then called for drinks all around. Two rounds later
he was crying. Talking about how Charlemagne
couldn't read but still made a world. About Hagia
Sophia and putting a round dome on a square
base after nine hundred years of failure.
The hand holding him slipped and he fell.
"White stone in the white sunlight," he said
as they picked him up. "Not the great fires
built on the edge of the world." His voice grew
fainter as they carried him away. "Both the melody
and the symphony. The imperfect dancing
in the beautiful dance. The dance most of all."

THE SPELL CAST OVER

In the old days we could see nakedness only
in the burlesque houses. In the lavish
theaters left over from vaudeville,
ruined in the Great Depression. What had been
grand gestures of huge chandeliers
and mythic heroes courting the goddess
on the ceiling. Now the chandeliers were grimy
and the ceilings hanging in tatters. It was
like the Russian aristocrats fleeing
the Revolution. Ending up as taxi drivers
in Paris dressed in their worn-out elegance.
It was like that in the Pittsburgh of my days.
Old men of shabby clothes in the empty
seats at the Roxy Theater dreaming
of the sumptuous headliners
slowly discarding layers of their
lavish gowns. Baring the secret
beauty to the men of their season.
The old men came from their one room
(with its single, forbidden gas range)
to watch the strippers. To remember what used
to be. Like the gray-haired men of Ilium
who waited each morning for Helen
to cross over to the temple in her light raiment.
The waning men longed to escape from the spell
cast over them by time. To escape the imprisoned
longing. To insist on dispensation. To see

their young hearts just one more time.
Those famous women like honeycombs. Women moving
to the old music again. That former grace of flesh.
The sheen of them in the sunlight, to watch
them walking by the sea.

SOUTH

For Susan Crosby Lawrence Anderson

In the small towns along the river
nothing happens day after long day.
Summer weeks stalled forever,
and long marriages always the same.
Lives with only emergencies, births,
and fishing for excitement. Then a ship
comes out of the mist. Or comes around
the bend carefully one morning
in the rain, past the pines and shrubs.
Arrives on a hot fragrant night,
grandly, all lit up. Gone two days
later, leaving fury in its wake.

He wonders why he can't remember the blossoming.
He can taste the brightness of the sour-cherry trees,
but not the clamoring whiteness. He was seven in
the first grade. He remembers two years later when
they were alone in those rich days. He and his sister
in what they called kindergarten.
They played every day on the towering
slate roofs. Barefoot. No one to see them on
those fine days. He remembers the fear
when they shot through the copper-sheeted
tunnels through the house. The fear
and joy and not getting hurt. Being tangled
high up in the mansion's Bing cherry tree with
its luscious fruit. Remembers
the lavish blooming. Remembers the caves they
built in the cellar, in the masses of clothing and draperies.
Tunnels to each other's kingdom with their stolen
jewelry and scarves. It was always summer, except for
the night when his father suddenly appeared. Bursting
in with crates of oranges or eggs, laughing in a way
that thrilled them. The snowy night behind him.
Who never brought two pounds of anything. The boy remembers
the drunkenness but not how he felt about it,
except for the Christmas when his father tried to embrace
the tree when he came home. Thousands of lights,
endless tinsel and ornaments. He does
not remember any of it except the crash as his father
went down. The end of something.

DREAMING AT THE BALLET

The truth is, goddesses are lousy in bed.
They will do anything it's true.
And the skin is beautifully cared for.
But they have no sense of it. They are
all manner and amazing technique.
I lie with them thinking of your
foolish excess, of you panting
and sweating, and your eyes after.

ELEGY

The bird on the other side of the valley
sings *cuckoo cuckoo* and he sings back, inside,
knowing what it meant to the Elizabethans.
Hoping she is unfaithful now. Delicate
and beautiful, making love with the Devil
in his muggy bedroom behind the shabby office.
While he is explaining the slums were there
when he got the job. *And* the Buicks burning
by the roads in the dark. He was not the one
doing the judging, he says. Or the one pointing down
at the lakes of burning lead. He is feeding
her lemons. Holding shaved ice in his mouth
and sucking her nipples to help with the heat.

AFTER LOVE

He is watching the music with his eyes closed.
Hearing the piano like a man moving
through the woods thinking by feeling.
The orchestra up in the trees, the heart below,
step by step. The music hurrying sometimes,
but always returning to quiet, like the man
remembering and hoping. It is a thing in us,
mostly unnoticed. There is somehow a pleasure
in the loss. In the yearning. The pain
going this way and that. Never again.
Never bodied again. Again the never.
Slowly. No undergrowth. Almost leaving.
A humming beauty in the silence.
The having been. Having had. And the man
knowing all of him will come to the end.

WAITING AND FINDING

While he was in kindergarten, everybody wanted to play
the tom-toms when it came time for that. You had to
run in order to get there first, and he would not.
So he always had a triangle. He does not remember
how they played the tom-toms, but he sees clearly
their Chinese look. Red with dragons front and back
and gold studs around that held the drumhead tight.
If you had a triangle, you didn't really make music.
You mostly waited while the tambourines and tom-toms
went on a long time. Until there was a signal for all
triangle people to hit them the right way. Usually once.
Then it was tom-toms and waiting some more. But what
he remembers is the sound of the triangle. A perfect,
shimmering sound that has lasted all his long life.
Fading out and coming again after a while. Getting lost
and the waiting for it to come again. *Waiting* meaning
without things. Meaning love sometimes dying out,
sometimes being taken away. Meaning that often he lives
silent in the middle of the world's music. Waiting
for the best to come again. Beginning to hear the silence
as he waits. Beginning to like the silence maybe too much.

WINTER HAPPINESS IN GREECE

The world is beyond us even as we own it.
It is a hugeness in which we climb toward.
A place only the wind knows, the kingdom
of the moon which breathes a thousand years
at a time. Our soul and the body hold each other
tenderly in their arms like Charles Lamb
and his sister walking again to the madhouse.
Hand in hand, tears on their faces, him carrying
her suitcase. Blow after blow on our heart
as we grope through the flux for footholds,
grabbing for things that won't pull loose.
They fail us time after time and we slide back
without understanding where we are going.
Remembering how the periodic table of the elements
didn't fit the evidence for half a century.
Until they understood what isotopes were.

MEANWHILE

It waits. While I am walking through the pine trees
along the river, it is waiting. It has waited a long time.
In southern France, in Belgium, and even Alabama.
Now it waits in New England while I say grace over
almost everything: for a possum dead on someone's lawn,
the single light on a levee while Northampton sleeps,
and because the lanes between houses in Greek hamlets
are exactly the width of a donkey loaded on each side
with barley. Loneliness is the mother's milk of America.
The heart is a foreign country whose language none
of us is good at. Winter lingers on in the woods,
but already it looks discarded as the birds return
and sing carelessly; as though there never was the power
or size of December. For nine years in me it has waited.
My life is pleasant, as usual. My body is a blessing
and my spirit clear. But the waiting does not let up.

THE ABUNDANT LITTLE

We have seen the population of Heaven
in frescoes. Dominions and unsmiling saints
crowded together as though the rooms were small.
We think of the grand forests of Pennsylvania,
oaks and maples, when we see the miniatures
of blue Krishna with farm girls awkwardly
beside a pond in a glade of scrub trees.
The Japanese scrolls show mostly Hell.
When we read about the Christian paradise,
it is made of gold and pearls, built on
a foundation of emeralds. Nothing soft
and rarely trees, except in the canvases
of Italians where they slip in bits of Tuscany
and Perugino's Umbria. All things
are taken away. Indeed, indeed.
But we secretly think of our bodies
in the heart's storm and just after.
And the sound of careless happiness.
We touch finally only a little.
Like the shy tongue that comes fleetingly
in the dark. The acute little that is there.

WORTH

It astonished him when he got to Kathmandu to hear
the man from the embassy say a friend was waiting
outside of customs. It was the Australian woman
he had met in Bali. His fault for running back
across the tarmac when he realized she was crying.
Kissing her while the plane waited with the door open.
Wanting her to feel valuable. Now she had used up all
her money flying to Nepal. In trouble because
we can't parse the heart. Calling what had been
what it was not. Now lying awkwardly on the bed
for a month, marooned in the heat, the Himalayas
above the window. As he watched the delicate dawns
and the old women carrying too much firewood down
from the mountain on their backs. Him thinking of their
happiness up in the lush green terraces of rice.
Remembering her laughter as he came out of the shower,
saying the boy had come again with a plate of melon.
"He asked if you were my husband," she said, "and I
said you were my father." Her eyes merry. Now they sat
in cheap restaurants trying to find anything to say.
Remembering how beautiful she was the first time
coming through the palm trees of the compound at dusk.
Tall and thin in a purple dress that reached to her
bare feet. Watching while he played chess with
the Austrian photographer all night. Now calling
that good thing by the wrong name. Destroying
something valuable. Innocently killing backwards.

PERFECTED

In the outskirts of the town
the street sweeper puts down
his broom of faggots and angrily
begins to shake the young ginkgo.
The leaves fall faster.
He shakes it even harder
and the leaves fall by ones and twos.
He rests to calm himself.
A passing boy speeds up
and leaps in the air,
slamming the trunk with both feet.
The yellow leaves spurt out.
The three of them stand looking up.
One leaf falls, then more.

LIVING HUNGRY AFTER

The water nymphs who came to Poseidon
explained how little they desired to couple
with the gods. Except to find out
whether it was different, whether there was
a fresh world, another dimension in their loins.
In the old Pittsburgh we dreamed of a city
where women read Proust in the original French,
and wondered whether we would cross over
into a different joy if we paid a call girl
a thousand dollars for a night. Or an hour.
Would it be different in kind or only
tricks and apparatus? I worried that a great
love might make everything else an exile.
It turned out that being together
at twilight in the olive groves of Umbria
did, indeed, measure everything after that.

THE MISTAKE

There is always the harrowing by mortality,
the strafing by age, he thinks. Always defeats.
Sorrows come like epidemics. But we are alive
in the difficult way adults want to be alive.
It is worth having the heart broken,
a blessing to hurt for eighteen years
because a woman is dead. He thinks of long
before that, the summer he was with Gianna
and her sister in Apulia. Having outwitted
the General, their father, and driven south
to the estate of the Contessa. Like an opera.
The fiefdom stretching away to the horizon.
Houses of the peasants burrowed into the walls
of the compound. A butler with white gloves
serving chicken in aspic. The pretty maid
in her uniform bringing his breakfast each
morning on a silver tray: toast both light
and dark, hot chocolate and tea both. A world
like *Tosca*. A feudal world crushed under
the weight of passion without feeling.
Gianna's virgin body helplessly in love.
The young man wild with romance and appetite.
Wondering whether he would ruin her by mistake.

A FACT

The woman is not just a pleasure,
nor even a problem. She is a meniscus
that allows the absolute to have a shape,
that lets him skate however briefly
on the mystery, her presence luminous
on the ordinary and the grand. Like the odor
at night in Pittsburgh's empty streets
after summer rain on maples and sycamore.
As well as the car suddenly crossing two blocks
away in a blare of light. The importance
of the rocks around his Greek shepherd hut,
and mules wandering around in the empty fields.
He crosses the island in the giant sunlight,
comes back in the dark thinking of the woman.
The fact of her goes on, loved or not.

BECOMING REGARDLESS

I begin to see them again as the twilight darkens.
Gathered below me and to the right under the tree.
Ghosts are by their nature drawn to the willows.
They have no feet and hover just above the grass.
They seem to be singing. About apples, I think,
as I remember the ones a children's red in the old
cemetery in Syracuse where I would eat one each day
because the tree grew out of a grave and I liked
to think of someone eating what was left of my heart
and spirit as I lay in the dark earth translating
into fruit. I can't be sure what they are singing
because no sound comes through the immense windows
of my apartment. (Except for the sound somebody
makes at two and four in the night as he passes
around what was the temple grounds hitting a block
of wood two or three times with a stick. I have
begun listening for it as I lie on the floor awake.)
I try to see in what is left of the light down there
the two I was. The ghost of the boy in high school
just before I became myself. The other is the ghost
of the times later when I could fall in love:
the first time, and three years after that for eight
years, and the last time ten years after. I feel
a great tenderness for all the dozen ghosts down
there trying to remain what they were. Behind each
pile of three boulders that are the gravestones
is a railing making an enclosure for the seven-foot,
narrow, unpainted planks with prayers written on them.
They are brought on the two ceremonial days each year
by the mourners and put with the earlier ones. But
in many enclosures there are just weathered old ones,
because they are brought only as long as there is
still someone who knew the dead. It puzzles me that

I care so much for the ghost of the boy in high school, since I am not interested in those times. But I know why the other one frightens me. He is the question about whether the loves were phantoms of what existed as appearance only. I know how easily they come, summoned by our yearning. I realize the luminosity can be a product of our heart's furnace. It would erase my life to find I made it up. Then I see them faintly dancing in the dark: spirits that are the invisible presence of what those women were. There once was a Venezia even if there is not now. The flesh thickens or wanes, but there was somebody I knew truly. Three of them singing under the willow inside my transience.

THE SECRET

There is an easy beauty in the bronze statues
dredged up from the ocean, but there is a worth
to the unshapely our sweet mind founders on.
Truth is like a pearl, Francis Bacon said.
It is lovely in clear light, but the carbuncle
is more precious because its deep red shows best
in varied illumination. "A mixture of a lie
doth ever add pleasure." When the Chinese made
a circle of stones on the top of their wells,
one would be a little skewed to make the circle
look more round. Irregularity is the secret
of music and to the voice of great poetry.
When a man remembers the beauty of his lost love,
it is the imperfect bit of her he remembers most.
The blown-up Parthenon is augmented by its damage.

THE NEW BRIDE ALMOST VISIBLE IN LATIN

We want to believe that what happens
in the dark bedroom is normal.
Pretending that being alive
is reasonable keeps the door shut
against whether maggots, nematodes,
and rot are also created in God's image.
Our excess is measured, our passion
almost deliberate. As we grow up,
we more and more love appropriately.
When Alicia got married, the priest
conducted the Mass in English because
it was understandable. He faced us
as though we were friends. Had us
gather around the altar afterwards.
She hugged and kissed each one until me.
The bride, fresh from Communion,
kissed me deeply with her tongue,
her husband three feet away.
The great portals of our knowing
each other closed forever. I was flooded
by the size of what had ended.
But it was the mystery of marriage
and its hugeness that shocked me,
fell on me like an ox. I felt
mortality mixing with the fragrance
of my intimacy with her. The difference
between the garden of her body
and the presence of her being was the same
distance as the clear English of the Mass from
the blank Latin which held the immensities.

THE DANGER OF WISDOM

We learn to live without passion.
To be reasonable. We go hungry
amid the giant granaries
this world is. We store up plenty
for when we are old and mild.
It is our strength that deprives us.
Like Keats listening to the doctor
who said the best thing for
tuberculosis was to eat only one
slice of bread and a fragment
of fish each day. Keats starved
himself to death because he yearned
so desperately to feast on Fanny Brawne.
Emerson and his wife decided to make
love sparingly in order to accumulate
his passion. We are taught to be
moderate. To live intelligently.

SEARCHING FOR IT IN A GUADALAJARA
DANCE HALL

You go in from the cobbled back street.
Into an empty, concrete one-room building
where prim youngish women sit in a line
of straight chairs. The women are wearing
tea dresses thrown away by rich Texan
women two generations ago. The men are
peasants, awkward in a line of chairs opposite.
Nothing is sexual. There are proprieties.
No rubbing against anyone. No touching
at all. When the music starts, the men
go stiffly over to the women. It isn't
clear whether they say anything. The dance is
a slow, solemn fox trot. When it stops,
they stand still while the men
find a coin. The women stow it and all
of them go back to the chairs to wait for
the music and another partner. This is
not for love. The men can get love
for two coins at a shack in the next field.
They know about that. And that they will
never be married, because it is impossible
to own even a little land. They are
groping for something else, but don't know what.

TRIANGULATING

All taken down like Trastevere or København.
Like her apartment on Waller in San Francisco
or their place on Oak. The ruined cities
of America. The grand theaters built for vaudeville,
tawdry and soiled when he knew
them in Baltimore and Chicago. Full of
raggedness and a band. Calumet City when
it was a mob town with public vice.
A scale visible in the decay. Something
to measure against. Night after night
walking the Paris he knew. Hôtel Duc de Bourgogne
on Île Saint-Louis, the room
with a stone floor on the rue Boutarel across from
the cathedral. The old building where
his mansard was on a hill above the canal.
All taken down. Places that were clues
for a moment when he understood.
Knew the name of our quarry.
The something we were changing into.

THE DIFFICULT BEAUTY

The air full of pictures no matter where you reach in.
Vast caverns in the ground bright with electricity
and covered everywhere with language. Because you
live on the fourth floor, you can on Sundays look
down into the synagogue across the street where people
sing secretly together in Spanish. You are up there
trying to get the galleys marked which are so late
(because of love) that Yale threatens not to publish
the book at all. Noise so loud you finally look
outside and see everybody gathered on Fourth Street
near Avenue C to eat ice cream and watch the guys
carrying a naked woman down the fire escape clumsily
who had been promising all morning to jump. But best
of all are the gardens: hidden places where they have
burned down the buildings and kept the soil
poor so the plants won't grow with vulgar abundance.
Like the Japanese gardens made only of rocks and sand
so their beauty would not be obscured by appearances.
Like the maharaja who set aside the best courtyards
in his palace for the dandelions he imported from
England to be kept alive by the finest gardeners
in the world who knew how to work against nature.

GROWING UP IN PITTSBURGH

Go down to the drugstore at the corner,
it said. At the drugstore it said,
Go to the old woman's house. On her porch
was scribbled: Where has love gone?
To the arcades of the moon, I wrote.
To the Palladian moon, and is embezzled
there as well. Therefore are the gunwales
of my heart plated. For the birds
have rings on their necks and must
take the catch to the white boats
at the marble pier in exchange for gruel.
Old hoplites cursing under the arcades
snap the pale fish and wrap them in plundered
drawings. A whimpering leaks from the bundles,
from the stalls, into the piazza and up
to the roof where everyone in the shining
is watching a performance of romance.

INFECTIOUS

I live with the sound my body is,
with the earth which is my daughter.
And the clean separation which is my wife.
There is no one who can control us
because we live secretly under the ocean
of each day. Except for the music.
The memory of rainy afternoons
in San Francisco when I would play
all the slow sections of Mozart's
piano concertos. And the sound
of the old Italian peasant who occasionally
came down from the mountain to play
a primitive kind of guttural bagpipe,
and sometimes sing with his broken voice
in the narrow lanes about the moon
and the grief of lovers. That reedy sound
is stuck in me. Like the Japanese monk
who would come through the graveyard
at night striking two sticks together.
I can't forget the pure sound I heard once
when a violin string snapped nearby
in three o'clock's perfect silence.
But I tell myself I'm safe. I remind myself
of the boy who discovered order in the piano
and ran upstairs to tell his little sister
that they didn't have to be afraid anymore.

PIECING OF THE LIFE

The man wondered if he had become
like Di Stefano, when he was no longer able
to sing the best of Verdi. He knew how better
than anyone, but finally didn't have the strength
for Othello. My friend's wife had left him
and he wondered if he could still hold the world
in his arms. And would he know if his quiet
was the beginning of decline. He talked often
of the first girl he kissed, when he was sixteen.
He had not been prepared for the velvety
plushness. We watched the evening begin.
"Fifty and waning," he said. Touched my arm and we
walked slowly back. Silent and wonderfully content.

NOT EASILY

When we get beyond beauty and pleasure,
to the other side of the heart (but short
of the spirit), we are confused about what
to do next. It is too easy to say arriving
is enough. To pretend the music
of the mountain needs only to be heard.
That the dance is known by the dancing,
and the lasagne is realized by eating it.
Not in this place on the other side
of desire. We can swim in the Aegean,
but we can't take it home. A man finds
a melon by the road and continues up
the hill thinking it is the warm melon
that will remain after he has forgotten
the ruins and sea of the summer. He tells
himself this even as the idea of the taste
is replacing what the melon tasted like.

He thought of the boy in the middle
of the poison gas. The gas mask dangerously
slipping on his face, because he was sweating
so much. ("Death on all sides.") Fear all through him,
but also the excitement from his intruding,
because of the privacy he had penetrated.
The hidden world he was not part of.
Glimpsed all his life in the windows he walked past
at night. The young mother dancing slowly
with her little daughter. The teenager preening
in her new dress in front of her father.
The world without him he was seeing as he
opened cupboards and pulled clothes
from the bureaus. Drawers of the daughter's
mysterious underclothes. What they had on
the dresser. Curiously the same as his rummaging
earlier in the refrigerator for the food
to put on the porch. Finding what had gotten
lost, shriveled, or spoiled. All his life wondering
what reality was, without his presence.
Lying in somebody's side lawn, the night rain
coming down and the smell of lilacs
as he watched a family eating dinner in their light.
Later the Hispanic women in the Laundromats.
And in Rome, when he lived with the peasants
from Calabria. Never a part of it
despite their friendship. Now in the village
of black magic with tokens among the trees
announcing which paths led to death. Trying
to decide about the Australian woman
beside him. The borders again, he thinks,
remembering the woman in København he had

never seen as he slid out of the terrible
cold into her sleepy warmth. Her face
invisible in the dark. The soft sound
she made welcoming him wordlessly,
utterly. Into the great light of her body.

CRUSOE ON THE MOUNTAIN GATHERING FAGGOTS

He gets dead sage and stalks of weeds mostly.
Oleander can kill a fire, they say.
The length of valley below is green
where the grapes are. The small farms
of wheat tiny. And two separate cows.
Then the sea. Here's a terraced mountain
abandoned to bracken and furze and not
even that. If there was water once,
there isn't now. Rock and hammering sun.
He tastes all of it again and again,
his madeleine. He followed that clue
so long it grew faint. Which must account
for his happiness in this wrong terrain.

SUMMER AT BLUE CREEK, NORTH CAROLINA

There was no water at my grandfather's
when I was a kid and would go for it
with two zinc buckets. Down the path,
past the cow by the foundation where
the fine people's house was before
they arranged to have it burned down.
To the neighbor's cool well. Would
come back with pails too heavy,
so my mouth pulled out of shape.
I see myself, but from the outside.
I keep trying to feel who I was,
and cannot. Hear clearly the sound
the bucket made hitting the sides
of the stone well going down,
but never the sound of me.

GOING HOME

Mother was the daughter of sharecroppers.
And my father the black sheep of rich Virginia
merchants. She went barefoot until twelve.
He ran away with the circus at fourteen.
Neither one got through grammar school.
And here I am in the faculty toilet
trying to remember the dates of Emperor Vespasian.

GETTING IT RIGHT

Lying in front of the house all
afternoon, trying to write a poem.
Falling asleep.
Waking up under the stars.

ALONENESS

Deep inside the night on the eighth floor.
Scared to be alone with him in his room.
Hoping the drug still controls his violence.
The massiveness of him. The girth
of the wrist as he holds it. And the sound
of his heart. In the corridor outside,
blank eyes at each of the small windows.
The silence getting denser and denser
as it continues farther away.

Everywhere the sighing of the beds
rocking slowly, steadily, eternally
in the hushed dimness as he reaches in
to the hot bed of the contagious fat woman
to turn her over. Him frightened in
the paper clothes and a mask.

They give him a dead woman swathed
tightly in loop after loop of brown tape,
from the crown of her head down
to the toes. Like a mummy under water.
Wrestling with it in the concrete basement.
The weight of her slack body pulling
out of his arms. Lifting her with difficulty
by hugging the body against him. Shocked
at the dead thing's heat. Fighting to get
her into the immaculate drawer. The sound
of steel sliding on steel.

The straight-edge razors they use on Saturday nights slash so fast and clean there is no pain. They fight on without noticing the mutilation. Ears gone, noses carved, cheeks laid bare. Standing in line later to be neatly staunched and stitched.

FEELING HISTORY

Got up before the light this morning
and went through the sweet damp chill
down to the mindlessly persisting sea.
Stood neck-deep in its strength thinking
it was the same water young Aristotle
knew before he stopped laughing.
The cold waves came in on me,
came in as the sun went from red
to white. All the sea turned blue
as I walked back past the isolate
shuttered villa.

TO KNOW THE INVISIBLE

The Americans tried and tried to see
the invisible Indians in the deeper jungle
of Brazil. Finally they put things in the clearing
and waited. They waited for months,
maybe for years. Until a knife and a pot
disappeared. They put out other things
and some of those vanished. Then one morning
there was a jungle offering sitting on the ground.
Gradually they began to know the invisible
by the jungle's choices. Even when nothing
replaced the gifts, it was a kind of seeing.
Like the woman you camp outside of, at the five portals.
Attending the conduits that tunnel from the apparatus
down to the capital of her. Through the body
and its weather, to the mind and heart, to the spirit
beyond. To the mystery. And gradually to the ghosts
coming and leaving. To the difference between
the nightingale and the Japanese nightingale
which is not a nightingale. Getting lost in the treachery
of language, waylaid by the rain dancing its pavane
in the bruised light of winter afternoons.
By the flesh, luminous and transparent in the silent
clearing of her. Love as two spirits flickering
at the edge of meeting. An apartment on the third
floor without an elevator, white walls and almost
no furniture. Water seen through pine trees.
Love like the smell of basil. Richness beyond
anyone's ability to cope with. The way love is after fifty.

PROSPERO GOES HOME

It was not difficult to persuade the captain
to sail a little off course and leave him
at the island. With his boxes on the sand
and the ship getting small, he was home.
Foolishly, he was disappointed that Ariel
was not amazingly there to meet him.
A part had secretly dreamed it would be a woman.
But that lasted briefly and then he was happy.
How dear the bare place looked. How good it felt
getting the supplies up to the house.

NAKED WITHOUT INTENT

She takes off her clothes without excitement.
Her eyes don't know what to do. There is silence
in the countries of her body, Umbrian hill towns
under those small ribs, foreign voices singing
in the distance of her back. She is invisible
under the glare of her nudity. Somewhere there
is a table and the chairs she will go back to.
These men will never know what station the radio
is already set on. She will leave soon and find
herself walking in the streets with the few
people who are still awake. She will enter
her room tired and a little confused by the night.
Confused by their seeing her utterly, seeing
everything but the simple fact of her. Tomorrow
she will be in a supermarket buying potatoes
and milk, mostly naked under her dress and maybe
different. Strangers around the city will know
the delicate colors of her nipples. Some will
remember her long feet. Will she feel special
now as she sets the alarm? Is there a danger she
might feel that nothing significant happened?

TRYING

Our lives are hard to know. The gardens are provisional,
and according to which moment. Whether in the burgeoning
of July or the strict beauty of January. The language
itself is mutable. The word *way* is equally an avenue
and a matter of being. Our way into the woods
is according to the speed. To stroll into loveliness,
or leaves blowing so fast they would shred
birds in an explosion of blood. It's the Devil's
mathematics that Blake spoke of, which I failed
all three times. Everyone remembers the wonderful day
in Canada when the water was perfect. I remember
the Italian afternoon when I carried Gianna on my shoulders
in the pool, her thighs straining around my head.
My falling awkwardly and getting water in my nose.
The embarrassment forty-nine years ago which I have rejoiced in.
"To war with a god-lover is not war," Edith Hamilton wrote,
"it is despair." What of the terribly poor Monet
scrounging for the almost empty tubes of paint his students
left. Or Watteau dying so long near Versailles. Always
the music of the court and the taste of his beautiful
goddesses constantly going away.

THE ANSWER

Is the clarity, the simplicity, an arriving
or an emptying out? If the heart persists
in waiting, does it begin to lessen?
If we are always good does God lose track
of us? When I wake at night, there is
something important there. Like the humming
of giant turbines in the high-ceilinged stations
in the slums. There is a silence in me,
absolute and inconvenient. I am haunted
by the day I walked through the Greek village
where everyone was asleep and somebody began
playing Chopin, slowly, faintly, inside
the upper floor of a plain white stone house.

The bright green of the flat fields stretching away
endlessly under the procession of great white clouds.
A ceremony without punctuation. The land empty
except for the way Chief Joseph ended just short
of the Canadian border.
                              He did not talk to them
about that, or how the tribe dwindled away amid
the immaculate silence. (As we did after
leaving college.) He did not talk to the young
about sweat lodges, or the pipe ceremony. He talked
about how America was born from the size around them,
the American mind and its spirit shaped by that
scale. They said it was just distance for them.
And boredom. How small it made them feel.

He asked about their old poetry, saying he could
not understand how it worked. They said they had never
read any of that. He talked about imagination,
as something hard. He began to hear their minds flickering.

An old woman showed him the big photographs she had
bought from the government of their great men.
She said she was one of the last three people who could
speak the language, and she would die soon. He felt
the doom everywhere. They were like a kind of whale
that was so scant it could never replace itself.
Hearing about the drunkenness and drugs and incest
each day. Then the amazing stars at night. Riding
around all day with the woman from the foundation
that had brought him there. Getting to know her
as they roamed through the ideal landscape. Lunch
and dinner together all the time. She talking about
her Irish family and growing up in New York. About

the man she lived with. Getting somebody to take
their picture. His heart flickering. His surprise.
His heart that had retired, safe in ripeness, hidden
in the light. Standing together in the terminal,
her plane straight ahead, his to the left. Both of them
stranded without a language for it.

WAKING AT NIGHT

The blue river is gray at morning
and evening. There is twilight
at dawn and dusk. I lie in the dark
wondering if this quiet in me now
is a beginning or an end.

CHERISHING WHAT ISN'T

Ah, you three women whom I have loved in this
long life, along with the few others.
And the four I may have loved, or stopped short
of loving. I wander through these woods
making songs of you. Some of regret, some
of longing, and a terrible one of death.
I carry the privacy of your bodies
and hearts in me. The shameful ardor
and the shameless intimacy, the secret kinds
of happiness and the walled-up childhoods.
I carol loudly of you among trees emptied
of winter and rejoice quietly in summer.
A score of women if you count love both large
and small, real ones that were brief
and those that lasted. Gentle love and some
almost like an animal with its prey.
What is left is what's alive in me. The failing
of your beauty and its remaining.
You are like countries in which my love
took place. Like a bell in the trees
that makes your music in each wind that moves.
A music composed of what you have forgotten.
That will end with my ending.

Not for rhyme or reason, but for the heart's sweet seasons and her perfect back sleeping in the morning dark.

SUDDENLY ADULT

The train's stopping wakes me.
Weeds in the gully are white
with the year's first snow.
A lighted train goes
slowly past absolutely empty.
Also going to Fukuoka.
I feel around in myself
to see if I mind. Maybe
I am lonely. It is hard
to know. It could be
hidden in familiarity.

The body is the herb,
the mind is the honey.
The heart, the heart is
the undifferentiated.
The mind touches the body
and is the sun.
The mind touches the heart
and is music.
When body touches heart
they together are the moon
in the silently falling snow
over there. Which is truth
exceeding, is the residence,
the sanctified, is the secret
closet and passes into glory.

UNCOLLECTED

POEMS

VALLEY OF THE OWLS

Night rises up from the fields
as the stars gather. Under the earth
are the stones and holding the stones
together is the silence. His heart
smelling of the cypress tree.
The whole valley at dawn sweet
with its emptiness. There is a door
in the wind, lima bean soup on the stove.
Tomorrow begins in the dark.
Today is the mountain of what we have
become. Surprised to be alive
in the abundance of time. Two thousand
six hundred and twenty days,
four thousand nights another time.
The red on the large woodpecker
four times in the pine trees.
The hoopoe in the chinaberry tree
only once. Wang Wei in his loneliness
noticing the first raindrops
in the light dust.

The silence around the old villa
was magnified by the shrilling
cicadas. Her soft voice redoubled
that stillness. At night the two
kinds of owls did not consider
each other but together made
something. The small owl mewed
and the other said *dark . . . dark*.
How fine it was up there on
the mountain. How happy Michiko
was. She was perishing but did
not know it. I took care of her
body in ways that crossed over
the boundaries of politeness.
The white ship that crossed slowly
to the next island every noon
doubled the blue of the Aegean.
Her absence makes this New England
town completely visible and less.

SPRING

I call it exile, or being relegated.
I call it the provinces.
And all the time it is my heart.
My imperfect heart which prefers
this distance from people. Prefers
the half-meetings which cannot lead
to intimacy. Provisional friendships
that are interrupted near the beginning.
A pleasure in not communicating.
And inside, no despair or longing.
A taste for solitude. The knowledge
that love preserves freedom in always
failing. An exile by nature. Where,
indeed, would I ever be a citizen?

There was a small butcher shop in the North End
of Boston whose specialty was inferior foods.
Chicken feet and chicken heads. Gizzards, tripe
and beef hearts. Salty fatback and wet brains.
Prosperous people came from the suburbs to pay
too much for the food they ate in hard times.
The man living with difficulty in the winter woods
remembers as he looks at the fresh raccoon tracks
in the snow and wonders if they will tug at him
in the Mediterranean light, if he will write
about the classical bareness of cold and truth
while eating the suckling pig and fried bananas
of Indonesia. Will he miss the Mill River
with its slags of ice and the sound of crows
in the silence. Some years ago, a child was asked
whether he liked radio or television best. The boy
said radio, because the pictures were better.

WINTER HAPPINESS

Pride, pride, pride, pride, pride,
pride and happiness. Winter
and empty fields and beyond the trees
the Aegean. The night sky
bright in the puddles of this lane.
Such dear loneliness. Going along
to no man's clock. No one who knows
my middle name for a thousand miles.
My youth gone and death unable to find me.
Thinking back to childhood. Astonished
that I could find the way here.

MAY I, MAY I

Mother says,
Take two baby steps.
The eyes and inside the mouth,
nipples and naked feet.
Dreams lived and lost
as the great secret.

Mother may I, he says
and she lets him.

Cold rooms in Manhattan
and San Francisco.
First love for the second time.
All night every night
in coffeehouse and bar.
Poetry and painting,
hunger and movies,
disappointment and lies.
Happy and alone.

Take two baby steps,
Mother says. Spring and forest,
music and trains and owls.
Denise and Doris, Marie
and Moira, Anna and Valerie.

Ah, Mother, may I?
and she says You may.
A little success. Dinners

and famous names.
Then giant steps away
from all that.
From the simplicity.

Mother says, Take your heart
in both hands and squeeze
out darkness. You must take
scissor steps down
into longing and forgetting,
loneliness and fear.

Mother must I?
You must.
People's agony and the injustice.
Your aging and listening.
Sickness and death.
The imperfecting.

Mother, he says, there is arriving
down here. Enjoyment
more than excitement.
Having been and being.
Happiness and ripeness
for all the time there is.
Italy and Greece when they are
spoiled and splendid.

THE WINNOWING

Their daughter makes a noise like a giant fly.
The family brought her today for the threshing.
She grew up here until they moved to the village.
She takes me around to see the geranium sprigs
she tried to plant while I did the laundry.
With a circle of stones to make a house for each.
Grins when I dribble water on them obediently
where she points. She is twenty and misshapen
and cannot speak. Sits on the wall wearing pink,
rocking in the quiet sound of grain being sifted.
Shadows of my doves fly across the bright stones
as she looks down the valley singing and happy
in the late afternoon. A very big happiness I think.

The last year of my being young the way young people
mean young, I was living with a friend in Perugia,
one of those Italian towns made of towers and arches
and Etruscan walls. Down below was gentle Umbria
and summer was coming. Both of us were unhappy.
His love was in Austria and mine was in Berkeley,
and neither of them wanted us now. Every night
we sat in the kitchen at a marble table writing fine
hopeless letters to get them back. His wife cooked
and comforted us and went to bed about one when
we began decorating the envelopes. I would finish first
and take mine to the post office through the sleeping
ancient city. Usually about three in the morning.
Then I would go to the dark palazzo and stand looking
up at Gianna's bedroom window. When I got home,
his pretty letter would be leaning on the sugar bowl.
I would go quietly across their bedroom to my door.
She would be sitting up holding him in her arms,
watching me as I passed through the first light of dawn.

BLINDED BY SEEING

I was lying on the deck with my eyes closed.
Somewhere to the left the women's voices began
to change, the voice of one pushing the others.
She idly sang bits of old songs, laughing
as though not noticing. And began to clap,
accentuating the rhythm, crying out.
Her laughing became a gypsy laugh, though I could
hear a shyness underneath. I could hear how
she was as a girl when the men would have urged her on
until she danced, dazzling the whole village.
But these women fell silent. The men nearby
went on playing cards and she gradually stopped.
Later, when I went for tea, I returned that way
to see her spirit in its full-breasted body.
But there was only a group of old ladies
dressed in black, each like the others.

THE GREEK GODS DON'T COME IN WINTER

The Greek gods don't come in winter,
and seldom in person. They speak through
others. Even in summer. Their voices seem
far off and very fast. It's difficult also
because we can't trust the people who say
they are translating. When the gods come
in the dawn, there is soon the odor
of roses and warm linen. They sit in their
high-backed chairs and mostly watch
the children. Especially when they are
running and laughing. They applaud
by humming when we read our poems.
They hum differently when the poems
are about lights and parallel geologies
of the sea. But they hum most of all
when the poems are about distance and desire.

THE CARGO AND THE EQUITY

A man lies warm under the blankets in a house still
frozen by the night, trying to remember the dream.
A lovely Japanese lady with bare breasts in a palanquin.
It changed and he was crowded against a fat man while
talking with a young woman from California at a party
who was beginning to tell him what she believed.
"Honor rather than bravery for instance," she said.
(He can hear the slow freight passing through
the ruined cornfields down by the river.) Dreams are
mostly things that we let go. What memory really keeps
is the cargo, the equity we have in our life.
He remembers an almost full moon white in the pale
afternoon sky yesterday and the snow gleaming
in the silence of gray winter light. He thinks
of a bright New England window last week where
a young mother was singing with her children.
And the lighted window near Hampstead Heath years ago
where a naked adolescent girl was laughing sweetly
with a man who was probably her father, holding up
her pretty dress, getting ready to go dancing with
the boy she loved. Any of that heartbreaking abundance.

THE STOCKTON TUNNEL

Someone had left a door unlocked in the Stockton
Tunnel and I went through almost without thinking.
Inside was a vast construction of Byzantium.
It must fill all of San Francisco down there,
shining with beautiful stone light. The watchman
was drunk, and annoyed by something they'd done.
He began telling secrets about the Leader and the order
and imminent takeovers. Most of which I couldn't follow
because of the whispering and looking away.
He changed after we'd crawled out on the scaffolding.
Wanted to attach electrical things to my earlobes.
It mattered a lot to him. When I still refused,
he started yelling and kicking the towers.
Harder and harder until a dim moaning began below
and timid voices floating up the mighty names
of the Paleologi, frail and lovely on the damp, spoiled air.

HOLDING ON TO MY FRIEND

The funeral service was people getting up
in the church and saying wonderful things
about my friend. The next night, the family
and some others gathered in the West Village
condominium and told flattering stories.
His daughter said Dad was always fun to be with.
I knew him well for thirty years and he had
never been fun, unless you counted those times
he struggled stubbornly to get the hang of charm.

My friend was fat and mean and lonely.
He made lots of money and never got anything
he really wanted. Most unhappy man I ever met.
There was resentment and even dislike in his
love for me. But we managed, knowing that.
We would spend long evenings reviewing again
his first marriage. Then he'd make his speech
about therapy teaching him how to express anger.
Afterwards, we would sit sleepy and silent
in the lavishness, embarrassed by our tenderness.

When I dream of him now, years later, he's driving
me to the airport, or we are on Fifth Avenue
near Rockefeller Center with him explaining again
how to reach Columbus Circle. We stand on,
talking of nothing. Comfortable, as the snow
falls the way it did in the old Pittsburgh.

People complain about too many moons in my poetry.
Even my friends ask why I keep putting in the moon.
And I wish I had an answer like when Archie Moore
was asked by a reporter in the dressing room
after the fight, "Why did you keep looking in
his eyes, Archie? The whole fight you were
looking in his eyes." And old Archie Moore said,
"Because the eyes are the windows of the soul, man."

ARS POETICA

He tries to tell the doctor:
"My heart springs open and I see
there is a woods inside.
The trees are full of birds
but they are unable to sing."
It's a good sign, the doctor says.

"My body begins to shine
brighter and brighter.
In the center of the light
there is a transparent woman
yelling, *Go back! Go back!*"
The doctor says that's promising.

"No," he says, "all of you lie to me.
Like the night they came to get me
out of bed at four in the morning.
Because Marmarosa wouldn't play
anymore. Unless I was there, they said.

"It was one of those blind pig places
I remember. And he made something perfect.
Made an architecture with the piano.
Like one of those buildings by Palladio.
But when he came to my table he was
as crazy as before. Like after Los Angeles.

"We left and walked through the empty streets
of East Liberty afterwards. Just before
it got light, Dodo in pain and mumbling.
It's what you're good at they use
to destroy you he said."

The doctor says Dodo was feeling
a little down because they took
away his children. "No, no!" he insists.
"I remember what Dodo was like before
he went with the Dorsey band.
When we were in high school, he was
like everybody else. When I went
to have his father cut my hair
I could always hear Dodo in the other
room practicing Chopin."
Yes, of course, the doctor says.

"You don't understand. He was famous.
He was important. Parker and Gillespie
would still go over to the house
when they passed through town.
He invented that music with them.
Things mattered."

(The doctor does not say anything.
Calm yourself, something whispers
inside him. *We can go home now.*)

MENISCUS: OR HOW THE HEART MUST NOT BE TOO MUCH QUESTIONED

There is a film on water
which permits a glass to hold
more than it can hold.
If probed, the water breaks.
Before and after,
both are truly water. But
only one will support swans.

THE COMPANION

There is someone. Always the same
half block behind. Not a doppelgänger
or anything like that. Not dangerous
or angelic. Just a middle-aged man
with a thick face wearing an old coat.
But always furtively just out of sight.
He is often on ridges very high up
when I walk along the empty beach.
When I am in the bedrooms, he is
discreet. He waits in a doorway
to see her face in the streetlight
as we go by. There is neither sex
nor love between us, but he will
follow the girl home. He stays far back
and never speaks to them. Once
he even helped me when I got trampled.
Very efficient, but ambiguous.
Except for that, we have never met.
One day, when he had lost me, I saw him
following an old damaged woman.
But he returns to me. Without kindness
or threat. My life is beginning to list.
He occupies more and more importance.
Meaninglessly. Nothing to do with God
or fate. Actually a man. Rather stout.
And I can't make out his intentions.
I am terrified by his not wanting anything.

THE RING

They have Mary's wedding ring in the Cathedral.
I was eager to see it, but learned it is
kept fastened in a box which requires keys
carried by the district's three main officials.
The box is locked seven times in a chest
and the keys held by their chief guilds.
The chest is sealed in the wall of the nave,
thirty feet in the air. Stairs are built to it
just once a year. It is a very holy relic,
and I assumed they feared thieves. Today,
when I asked of it, I learned it is magic.
The color changes according to the soul before it.
Then I understood about the locks. The ring
is not being protected. It is locked in.

LUST

I have drifted into the habit
of going to Matins. Today
I found they are repairing
the church. The side windows
have been taken out. I was shocked
by the sound of swallows. By sun
and the smell of morning.
I realized there has been a mistake.

THE SIXTH MEDITATION: FACES OF GOD

It is convenient for the old men to blame Eve.
To insist we are damned because a country girl
talked to the snake one afternoon long ago.
Children must starve in Somalia for that,
and old women be abandoned in our greatest cities.
It's why we will finally be thrown into the lakes
of molten lead. Because she was confused
by happiness that first time anyone said
she was beautiful. Nevertheless, she must be
the issue, so people won't notice that rocks
and galaxies, mathematics and rust are also
created in His image.

                       The forest must
not show the other face: slugs and grubs,
nematodes, and greenhead flies laying eggs
so their white larvae squirm in the filth.
Tent caterpillars, high in the trees, swarm out
from their offensive shrouds to eat the green
luxury bare. Spiders cast their nets in the dark.
Aphids gorge on lice. The braconid wasps lay eggs
under the skin of sphinx caterpillars so the larvae
will bore their way out through the host.
The other faces of God are not mediated by our
heart's need. We are not stone, nor even jungle.
We are animals haunted by love. Not spirits
buried in flesh, but the flesh itself.
And the spirit we are is not separated from it.

There is a god who prepares the locust in the blind
earth for seventeen years, to have it born without
a mouth. I believe in the spirit that would have
Agamemnon sail home with Iphigenia alive in his arms,
leaving Helen with her young man.

If human love and God's love meet
There is where we'll find defeat.

When spirit and the flesh are twin
There is where we can begin.

Where the heart is not at rest
There will I build my only nest.

CONVALESCING

I spend the days deciding
on a commemorative poem.
Not, luckily, an epitaph.
A quiet poem
to establish the fact of me.
As one of the incidental faces
in those stone processions.
Carefully done.
Not claiming that I was
at any of the great victories.
But that I volunteered.

NOTES

Some of these poems have been revised since their initial appearance in book form. Most of the changes are minor, involving spelling or punctuation.

In *Views of Jeopardy*, the first letter of each line was originally capitalized, a tradition abandoned when poems from this collection were reprinted in *Monolithos*.

The epigraph to "Portolano" is Sanskrit, meaning "In some place is a city."

The first section of *Monolithos* originally included sixteen poems previously published in *Views of Jeopardy*. These were "In Dispraise of Poetry," "Perspective He Would Mutter Going to Bed," "And She Waiting," "It May Be No One Should Be Opened," "Rain," "County Musician," "Orpheus in Greenwich Village," "Don Giovanni on His Way to Hell (II)," "Before Morning in Perugia," "The Night Comes Every Day to My Window," "The Abnormal Is Not Courage," "Susanna and the Elders," "I'll Try to Explain About the Fear," "New York, Summer" (originally titled "Portrait Number Five: Against a New York Summer"), "On Growing Old in San Francisco," and "The Whiteness, the Sound, and Alcibiades."

"Spring," "Meniscus: Or How the Heart Must Not Be Too Much Questioned," "The Companion," "The Ring," "Lust," and "Convalescing" are drawn from a manuscript titled *Torches at Noon*, written in the early 1960s under a pseudonym.

INDEX OF TITLES

INDEX OF FIRST LINES

I was carrying supplies back up the mountain, 152
I was getting water tonight, 308
I was lying on the deck with my eyes closed, 370
I was walking through the harvested fields, 66
I went to sleep by the highway, 114
I woke up every morning on the fourth floor, 294
I worked my way up the terraced gardens behind the house, 90

Let's get hold of one of those deer, 157
Light is too bare, too simple for her. She has lived, 194
Love is apart from all things, 132
Love is like a garden in the heart, he said, 309
Lying in front of the house all, 343

Marrying is like somebody, 82
Maybe when something stops, something lost in us, 191
Meelee's away in Lima, 27
Mogins disliked everything about Anna's pregnancy, 169
Monolithos was four fisherman huts along the water, 63
More and more it is the incidental that makes, 301
Most nights he would be upstairs with the wife, 92
Mother says, 366
Mother was the daughter of sharecroppers, 342
My brother's girlfriend was not prepared for how much blood, 79

Night after night after hot night in the clearing, 188
Night rises up from the fields, 361
Not for rhyme or reason, but for the heart's, 356
Nothing here. Rock and fried earth, 230
Not the river as fact, but the winter river, 158
Not wanting to lose it all for poetry, 111
Now come the bright prophets across my life, 35

Obsidian. Sturgeon. Infatuated angels, 70
Of course it was a disaster, 136
Once upon a time I was sitting outside the café, 187
On Fish Mountain, she has turned away, 161
Only you and I still stand in the snow on Highland Avenue, 221

On the beach below Sperlonga everyone else is, 163
Orpheus is too old for it now. His famous voice is gone, 135
Our heart wanders lost in the dark woods, 273
Our lives are hard to know. The gardens are provisional, 350
Our slow crop is used up within an hour. So I live, 83
Out of money, so I'm sitting in the shade, 223

People complain about too many moons in my poetry, 375
Perhaps if we could begin some definite way, 57
"Perspective," he would mutter, going to bed, 4
Poem, you sonofabitch, it's bad enough, 252
Poetry is a kind of lying, 52
Pride, pride, pride, pride, pride, 365
Pure, 37

Robinson Crusoe breaks a plate on his way out, 113
Rotting herds everywhere on the outskirts, 101

She came into his life like arriving halfway, 284
She is never dead when he meets her, 281
She lives, the bird says, and means nothing, 209
She might be here secretly, 302
She takes off her clothes without excitement, 349
She told about when the American soldiers, 185
Sixteen years old, surrounded by beasts in the pens, 195
So I come on this birthday at last, 45
Someone had left a door unlocked in the Stockton, 373
Sorrow everywhere. Slaughter everywhere. If babies, 213
Suddenly this defeat, 15

That is what the Odyssey means, 297
The air full of pictures no matter where you reach in, 333
The air this morning is pleasant and praises nothing, 201
The Americans tried and tried to see, 347
The bird on the other side of the valley, 315
The birds do not sing in these mornings. The skies, 205
The blue river is gray at morning, 354
The boat of his heart is tethered to the ancient, 283

The body is the herb, 358
The boy came home from school and found a hundred lamps, 159
The brain is dead and the body is, 274
The bright green of the flat fields stretching away, 352
The Chinese, to whom the eighteenth-century English, 88
The classical engine of death moves my day. Hurrying me, 86
The couple on the San Francisco bus looked Russian, 97
The door was in the whitewashed eight-foot walls, 215
The fellow came back to rape her again last night, 91
The fish are dreadful. They are brought up, 123
The four perfectly tangerines were a, 31
The fox pushes softly, blindly through me at night, 138
The French woman says, Stop, you're breaking my dress, 80
The funeral service was people getting up, 374
The girl shepherd on the farm beyond has been, 257
The glare of the Greek sun, 233
The goldfish is dead this morning on the bottom, 210
The great foreign trees and turtles burn, 5
The great light within the blackness shines out, 67
The Greek fishermen do not, 299
The Greek gods don't come in winter, 371
The heat's on the bus with us, 247
The intricate vast process has produced, 289
Their daughter makes a noise like a giant fly, 368
The last year of my being young the way young people, 369
The Lord gives everything and charges, 263
The Lord sits with me out in front watching, 170
The man certainly looked guilty, 124
The man wondered if he had become, 336
The massive overhead crane comes, 216
The monks petition to live the harder way, 151
The night comes every day to my window, 26
The old women in black at early Mass in winter, 270
The orchard changed. His appetite drifted, 93
The oxen have voices, 21
The pigeon with a broken wing, 108
The Poles rode out from Warsaw against the German, 28
The provisional and awkward harp, 33

They piled the bound angels with the barley, 278
They were cutting the spring barley by fistfuls, 72
They will put my body into the ground, 96
Things that are themselves. Waves water, the rocks, 71
Think what it was like, he said. Peggy Lee and Goodman, 291
This monster inhabits no classical world, 10
This morning I found a baby scorpion, 206
Three days I sat, 23
Thrushes flying under the lake. Nightingales singing underground, 75
To tell the truth, Storyville was brutal. The parlors, 148
Trying to scrape the burned soup from my only pan, 207
Two days ago they were playing the piano, 17
Two girls barefoot walking in the rain, 39

Used, misled, cheated. Our time always shortening, 295

Walked around Bologna at three in the morning, 279
Walking home across the plain in the dark, 68
Walking in the dark streets of Seoul, 244
Watching my wife out in the full moon, 64
Watching the ant walk underwater along, 231
We are all burning in time, but each is consumed, 229
We are given the trees so we can know, 275
We are not one with this world. We are not, 268
We are resident inside with the machinery, 219
We are surrounded by the absurd excess of the universe, 293
We come from a deep forest of years, 267
We find out the heart only by dismantling what, 129
We had walked three miles through the night, 112
We have already lived in the real paradise, 232
We have seen the population of Heaven, 320
We learn to live without passion, 330
We stopped to eat cheese and tomatoes and bread, 178
We think of lifetimes as mostly the exceptional, 176
We think the fire eats the wood, 183
We think there is a sweetness concealed in the rain, 84
We want to believe that what happens, 329
We were talking about tent revivals, 78

Jack Gilbert is the author of five volumes of poetry. His many awards include the Yale Younger Poets prize, the National Book Critics Circle Award for Poetry, and the Los Angeles Times Book Prize. His second collection, *Monolithos*, was a finalist for the Pulitzer Prize. He served in various countries as a lecturer for the U.S. State Department and has taught at Rikkyo University (Tokyo), San Francisco State University, Smith College, and elsewhere.

A NOTE ON THE TYPE

This book was set in Janson, a typeface thought to have been
made by the Dutchman Anton Janson. It has been conclusively
demonstrated that these types are actually the work of Nicholas
Kis (1650–1702).

Composed by North Market Street Graphics, Lancaster, Pennsylvania

Printed and bound by Berryville Graphics, Berryville, Virginia

Designed by Maggie Hinders